VOICE OF THE SOUL

Anatomy of The Human Fabric Trilogy

By Andrew R. Sadock

A comprehensive series of books designed to guide you through virtually any routine or extraordinary situation, to help you navigate any relationship, and to reveal your unique life purpose and life service through a time-proven, ancient prescription.

A HOLISTIC GUIDE FOR EVERYDAY LIVING
150 ESSENTIAL LESSONS

An easy-to-read reference book presenting practical guidance for gracefully navigating contemporary situations based upon ancient wisdom. A pragmatic adaptation of the renowned book of Chinese Taoist wisdom, the *Tao Te Ching*, complemented by other visionary, inspiring philosophies and the author's experience as a practitioner in the realm of holistic (mind-body) energy-work.

CONSCIOUS RELATIONSHIP

Using a simple analogy based upon ancient philosophy, this book answers the following questions: What is the higher purpose of relationship? Why do we attract whom we attract? What keeps a couple together in the long run? The book illuminates how various factors (natural timing, intention, communication, and the mechanisms of the subconscious mind) affect relationship.

VOICE OF THE SOUL
A CALL TO ACTION

A synopsis of personal transformation. Three types of activity innately unlock access to the wisdom of the soul—via dreams, intuitions, and synchronicity—revealing one's unique life purpose and life service.

Voice of the Soul

A Call to Action

Anatomy of the Human Fabric Trilogy, Volume Three

ANDREW R. SADOCK

Wisdom Moon Publishing
2017

VOICE OF THE SOUL
A CALL TO ACTION

Anatomy of the Human Fabric, Volume Three

Copyright © 2017 Wisdom Moon Publishing LLC

Published by Wisdom Moon Publishing LLC
San Diego, CA, USA

Wisdom Moon™, the Wisdom Moon logo™, *Wisdom Moon Publishing* ™, and *WMP* ™
are trademarks of Wisdom Moon Publishing LLC.

www.WisdomMoonPublishing.com

ISBN 978-1-938459-41-2 (softcover, alk. paper)
ISBN 978-1-938459-44-3 (eBook)
LCCN 2017946406

DEDICATION

This trilogy is dedicated to my brother, Jonathan Robert Sadock.
Our time together, albeit too brief, continues to inspire my path.

I miss jamming on guitar and drums after school
and playing baseball with you, Johnny!
We had a lot of fun, eh?

Your sudden absence ripped me to pieces.
Then reassembled me molecule by molecule from the inside out.
But not without help from incredible teachers — whom I never sought.
Miraculously, somehow they found me. Thank God!
They taught mostly without words and led by example.
Guess I was deemed ready for them
as I'd landed in the sub-basement of existence.

I wish no one ever had to endure such an experience.
Yet this was the defining experience of my life.
All I do, all I think, all I say
is because of you and your path.
And, in turn, the teachers
who were graciously placed before me.

You taught me much. How to love. How to let go.
But only after learning the true nature of things.
That everything is impermanent.
That all situations are perfectly designed and timed
to help us evolve.

As my greatest teacher explained using words
but only after gifting me with a 5-hour transcendent journey,
a sacred inner trek which conveyed more than words could ever say:
"It's simply a 3-D movie. It's not real … except to the ego. [Know
that] all conditions are perfect" as they are designed to help us
transcend ego/monkeymind.

Thank you.

My dear brother, may your journey be filled with Light.

Table of Contents

ARE YOU SELF-AWARE?

ARE YOU AWARE … that you have a unique life purpose and life service – that are known to your soul (but not personality)?

ARE YOU AWARE … that you can open the (vertical) gateways to success, health, and enlightenment by utilizing the ancient technologies of guided language, sound (tone and phonics), visual cues, kinesthetic movement (self and administered), smell, taste, creativity, emotional release, and meditation?

ARE YOU AWARE … that there is more to a truly successful life than mere happiness – as joy and bliss are equally vital components of profound success?

ARE YOU AWARE … that you can achieve profound and comprehensive success by working smart, rather than merely by working hard?

ARE YOU AWARE … that you can actively attract guidance in the form of synchronicity, intuition, dreams … and miracles?

ARE YOU AWARE … that there are foreseeable ages at which your life shall change? For example, you gain profound depth of insight every 7 years, and you repeat unresolved lessons every 12 years. Additionally, it takes 90 DAYS to ascertain truth (develop trust) in new situations (i.e., in new relationships, jobs and other situations - at a subconscious level)?

ARE YOU AWARE … that meditation is 25 percent willingness, 25 percent surrender and 50 percent grace? You do not meditate. Rather, you are meditated (by grace).

Intellect is a wonderful servant, but a poor master.

Using ancient technology rather than intellect and contemporary methods, we can access the eternal wisdom of the soul (i.e., "gut feeling") – to discover our true path (life purpose and life service), evolve, and experience profound and comprehensive success in daily living.

Three types of activity inspire the soul, source of the voice of truth within, to reveal our unique life purpose and life service – via enhanced intuition, dreams, synchronicity and … miracles.

The subconscious mind creates two-thirds of worldly experience. Soul-aligned (vertical) activities pro-actively access and enrich the subconscious mind via five sensory gateways (vision, hearing, smell, taste, movement), extrasensory perception, and self-awareness – raising vibration of the inner landscape that, via the Law of Attraction, innately manifests profound success.

A 90-day program of soul-aligned activity will help you to more easily access the present moment – gateway to the wisdom of the soul, the vessel of core truth … and lasting abundance in the form of happiness, joy and bliss.

Words obviously cannot convey
The Wisdom imparted by experience.

The goal of every activity
Is to attain Wisdom.

Yet perhaps something in the words herein
Will inspire conscious action,
Subsequent experience
And, thus,
Attainment of Wisdom.

***

The Wisdom of verticality (soul-alignment) is both ancient and profound.

And somewhat obvious.

Consider the upright nature of human beings,
Whereas once we walked on all fours.

Consider the spine. The vertical core that defines health and strength.

Consider the vertical Himalayas.
Some say the most enchanted and sacred of lands.
Closest to Heaven.

Consider the vertical depths of greatest sea.
Gateway to an enchanted world.

Consider the Antahkarana, the Tibetan bridge to consciousness,
That spans from Heaven to Earth via the chakras,
On the wings of breath, intention and conscious activity.

Consider the meditator
Whose inner gaze
Is toward Heaven
Yet Earth.

THE BIG PICTURE
PERSONAL TRANSFORMATION

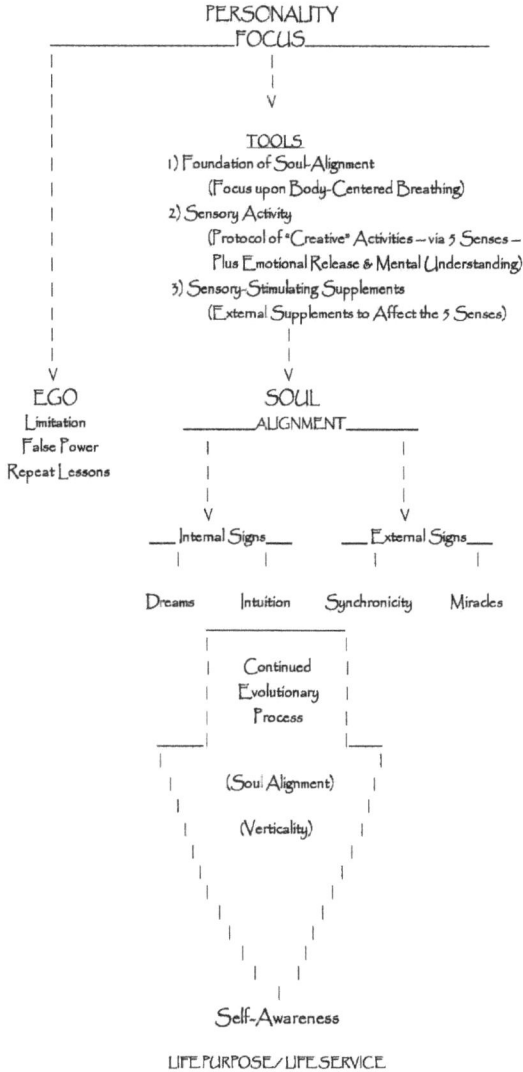

```
                          PERSONALITY
        _____FOCUS_____
        |                     |
        |                     |
        |                     V
        |
        |                   TOOLS
        |          1) Foundation of Soul-Alignment
        |                (Focus upon Body-Centered Breathing)
        |          2) Sensory Activity
        |                (Protocol of "Creative" Activities – via 5 Senses –
        |                 Plus Emotional Release & Mental Understanding)
        |          3) Sensory-Stimulating Supplements
        |                (External Supplements to Affect the 5 Senses)
        |                     |
        V                     V
      EGO                   SOUL
    Limitation       _____ALIGNMENT_____
    False Power        |                 |
    Repeat Lessons     |                 |
                       |                 |
                       V                 V
                 ___Internal Signs___   ___External Signs___
                       |                 |

      Dreams      Intuition      Synchronicity      Miracles
                       |                 |
                       |    Continued    |
                       |    Evolutionary |
                       |    Process      |
                  _____|                 |_____
                  |                           |
                  |      (Soul Alignment)     |
                  |                           |
                  |       (Verticality)       |
                  |                           |
                   |                         |
                    |                       |
                     |                     |
                      |                   |
                       |                 |
                        |               |
                         |             |
                          |           |
                           Self-Awareness

              LIFE.PURPOSE/LIFE.SERVICE
```

PREFACE

THIS BOOK presents the theoretical and practical foundation for a three-book series. *Voice of the Soul: A Call to Action* succinctly describes the "big picture" (synopsis) of personal transformation. The book then prescribes three types of activity that serve to efficiently accelerate our evolution, eventually carrying us to self-awareness – defined herein as awareness of one's life purpose and life service.

We are a relatively undisciplined society. We "think" (over-analyze and pontificate) too much. The monkeymind is the enemy. It blocks the voice of the soul. It may be defeated by exercise of conscious activity.

The big picture of personal transformation may be described as a simple flow-chart. The ancient Taoists believed that what we focus upon in each moment is all that we are, as all that exists is the moment. This moment. This moment. And this moment, ad infinitum. Our focus in this dualistic world is binary. Either we focus upon ego (the automatic default position) or soul. We focus upon (i.e., align with) the wisdom of the soul by employing three types of "conscious" activity.

When aligned with the soul, by using such conscious activity, the soul sends us signs to affirm our connection to the soul (and what the Taoists describe as Heaven and Earth). The soul speaks to us internally through enhanced dreams and intuition, and communicates with us externally via synchronicity and . . . miracles. The information received from the soul guides us to further conscious (soul-aligned) activity – a positive feedback loop – and ultimately helps to innately reveal our life purpose and life service – information that cannot be gleaned via the "thinking" mind.

"The world illusion, maya, ignorance,
delusion [confusion of the mind]
can never be destroyed

through intellectual conviction
or analysis [by the mind]
but solely through attaining the interior state
of nirbikalpa samadhi
[self-realization; profound self-awareness;
connection to natural order.]"
— Paramahansa Yogananda
Autobiography of a Yogi

You cannot defeat
the confusion and limitation of the mind
With the mind.
A timeless lesson.

The different sensory stimuli to which [hu]man[s] react[s] –
Tactual, visual, gustatory, auditory, and olfactory –
Are produced by vibratory variations in electrons and protons.
The vibrations in turn are regulated by "lifetrons,"
Subtle life forces or finer-than-atomic energies
Intelligently charged
[By conscious intention and unconscious landscape.]

[To consciously create, one must be able
To] tun[e] himself with the [life] force
By [using] certain [soul-aligned, vertical] practices
[And thereby] able to guide the lifetrons
To re-arrange their vibratory structure
[To] objectivize the desired result
[As long as aligned with the will of natural order.]

— Paramahansa Yogananda
Autobiography of a Yogi

We create our world experience
In every moment
Whether we realize this truth or not.
Create by default

3

Or consciously create.
A choice we make in each moment.

Soul is a great teacher
For it guides us to higher ground
Via intuition, dreams, synchronicity . . . & miracles.
Yet, we are the soul for soul is true self.
Thus, we guide ourselves.
Learn how to tap highest guidance.

"Except ye see signs and wonders, ye will not believe."
                                                    — John 4:48

Aligned with Soul
Our True Path
Is Illuminated

By Intuition
By Synchronicity
By Dreams
And
By Miracles

Aligned with Soul
We are Guided
By an Inner Knowing

To Happiness
To Joy
And
To Bliss

Aligned with Soul
The Monkey Mind
The Confused and Limited Personality
Which Otherwise Resists Truth
Every Step of the Way
Is Bypassed
And Ultimately Dissolved

Be Aware
And Know
This is True

"Be Vertical . . . Dissolve."

— Chris H.

DEDICATION

*"When the student is ready
the teacher appears."*

This book is dedicated to my brother, Jonathan Robert Sadock, and to my parents, family, friends, and the following guides who helped shape my life. First and foremost, I am thankful to a great Master (who prefers to remain anonymous). At age thirty I was fortunate to be presented with an experience that ultimately altered the course of my life. This unsought, synchronous event centered upon a surprise visit with this energetic master, and a subsequent five-hour journey into deep meditation (in which I experienced certain phenomena that are typically described as common elements of "near death experiences"). Prior to this visit I was not merely wholly ignorant but, in fact, was pervasively skeptical regarding the validity of any concepts and philosophies outside the jurisdiction of contemporary Western, empirically-based, allopathic medicine, psychology and philosophy. I am eternally grateful for this inner trek. This experience opened my previously closed mind to the possibility of the legitimacy and value of alternative philosophies, paradigms, and methodologies regarding life and its intricacies – perhaps most succinctly described as "holistic awareness" [self-awareness and energetic (a/k/a vibrational) medicine] and emotional intelligence. He showed me what is possible. And how to get there (by choosing to be vertical in each moment).

In subsequent years I inadvertently met three adept beings. First, a renowned Taoist Qi Gong teacher (T'ai Chi is a form of Qi Gong) and practitioner named Bruce Kumar Frantzis. Kumar is the adopted son of Liu Hung Shieh, an enlightened Taoist monk living in the Shao Lin Temple in Beijing, China. Kumar was America's first T'ai Chi fighting champion and evolved to become a master of the water method of Qi Gong. I met Kumar at Esalen Institute during my tenure there as an energyworker and resident, while sitting in a hot tub on a cliff overlooking the Pacific Ocean. He taught a Qi Gong workshop that evening. The next morning, following breakfast, he invited me to reside in his home north of San Francisco to study Qi Gong and Nei Gong ("internal energy arts") practice. Thereafter, I was invited to meditate and informally study with Tibetan lama Arjia Rinpoche. Lama Rinpoche is singly devoted to "right activity" in every moment – as though his mantra.

Finally, I engaged in meditation and chanting at Midwest Buddhist Temple in Chicago with Reverend Koshin Ogui. Reverend Ogui is a realist who advocates clarity, seeing things as they truly are. He encourages openness to the "impact" of life – suggesting that we embrace the lessons learned from both the ups and downs of life's rhythm. He teaches students to maintain self-awareness as though through the eyes of an outside observer, especially while in the throes of crisis. I am grateful to each teacher for the guidance, kindness, and generosity extended to me.

* * *

HOW TO READ THIS BOOK

The material presented in this text is holistic by nature. The concepts described herein are intimately entwined, interconnected and progressive. The material may seem repetitive – yet it builds upon itself. So, if you read a section that doesn't seem to make much sense, or which seems to lack detail – don't fret. Rather, read on – as the concept will likely be discussed in enhanced detail later in the text.

Chapter One

THE SELF

PERSONALITY & SOUL

THE SELF IS MORE THAN JUST PERSONALITY. The self is comprised of two distinct components – namely, personality and soul (ignoring the bodymind for the moment – which shall be discussed in detail later in the book).

PERSONALITY: The personality is the profane (uninspired, mundane, everyday, typical, technical, automatic and/or robotic) aspect of self that takes care of routine tasks and even certain seemingly quasi-complex tasks – in an uninspired, relatively unconscious, *unintuitive* manner. Such tasks may include driving a car, cleaning, laundering, watching television, completing technical homework, reading a tabloid, using the telephone, routine multitasking, handling most aspects of any given job, applying pre-determined formulae, learning the technical aspects of playing a musical instrument, etc.

Just as a computer is a necessary tool in today's world, the personality is a necessary tool. We could not get by in the world without personality. *The primary responsibility and focus of the soul is upon inner evolution, activated by mastery of life lessons. The responsibility and focus of personality is upon accomplishment of tasks in the material world. By design it is the responsibility of the personality to be a reliable, capable and effective*

10

tool of the soul. In theory, the innately wise soul subtly or not-so-subtly tells the personality what to do, and personality's assistance helps the soul accomplish its mission in the material world. Unfortunately, the *unevolved* aspect of the personality prefers not to listen to the guidance of the soul and, instead, tries to block access to the wisdom of the soul. Herein lies one of the great challenges of self-evolution – the taming of the unbridled emotional and mental reactiveness of the unevolved aspect of the personality (a/k/a what the Taoists describe as "monkeymind.") **The soul's guidance to the personality takes the form of intuition, dreams, synchronicity and . . . miracles.** The unevolved aspect of the personality does its best to block access to these forms of soul communiqué.

Personality's focus is upon material accomplishment. **Personality, in simplest terms, consists of two aspects – the ego and a soul-guided component.** Ego is that aspect of the personality that seeks immediate gratification, short-term gain in the material world. Ego is the aspect of the personality that is referred to as the monkeymind – as it continuously squirms to achieve *certainty* (which does not exist in the dualistic world).

> *The monkeymind abhors uncertainty*
> *To thwart uncertainty*
> *The monkeymind takes any action necessary*
> *To obtain an illusory sense of control*

Ego/monkeymind despises uncertainty. Ego perceives uncertainty as its greatest nemesis. So, ego will do anything to alleviate or minimize *perceived* uncertainty. However, what ego doesn't realize, among other things, is that there are no certainties in life (in the dualistic world) – except for the absolute that is natural order (a/k/a highest inspiration, the Infinite, etc.). Ego relentlessly attempts to think any thought, speak any word, and take any action that it believes may ease perceived uncertainty. Even if the thought, word or action hurts us (i.e., slows the evolution of the soul) in the long-run. Certainly you have experienced instances in which your ego motivated you to think, say or do things that you subsequently regretted . . . such as making a rushed, near-sighted decision or saying hurtful things to another person, etc.

Of its own accord, personality hasn't a clue as to who you truly are. Personality doesn't know your true life purpose and life service. Only the soul is aware of your core truth.

PERSONALITY MAY BE ALIGNED OR UNALIGNED (WITH THE GUIDANCE OF THE SOUL). Personality is described as "aligned" when it acts in accordance with the guidance of the soul. *This occurs when we allow the soul-driven aspect of our personality, rather than ego, to be the focus and pilot of our personality's attention.* However, until an individual earns at least a modicum of self-awareness – i.e., until a person becomes somewhat *aware* of the competing agendas of the ego and soul – the personality is an unreliable tool for the soul to employ. **Rather than perform as a tool that assists the soul, the egoic aspect of the personality (i.e., ego) behaves as nemesis to the guidance of the soul.** The ego eternally attempts to overcome the wisdom of omnipresent soul so as to effectively block the soul from accomplishing its mission in the world.

The way to conquer the devastating potential of the ego is to bypass (and eventually dissolve) the ego's reactive thoughts and emotions, and unaligned materialistic desires (those desires that are not aligned with your core truth – life purpose and life service). **Soul-aligned (vertical) activities cause us to maintain focus aligned with the soul, rather than insidious ego. By definition, personality is "aligned" – with the energy and wisdom of the soul - when** *focused* **upon the soul, and unaligned when** *focused* **on the false perception of ego.** More will be discussed on this later.

THE UNALIGNED ASPECT OF THE PERSONALITY (EGO) IS A GREAT TRICKSTER. The unaligned personality/ego resists the guidance of the infinitely wise soul. Worse *yet, the unaligned personality tries to trick us into believing that it, rather than the soul, knows what is best for us (in the long-run). This couldn't be further from the truth.* . . .

The unaligned personality/ego acts like an out-of-control computer, reeking havoc upon anyone and anything it its path of its misguided thoughts, words, actions and reactionary thoughts and emotions. The ego then makes matters worse by trying to trick us into believing that this is appropriate behavior. The greatest danger created by the unaligned personality/ego is its extraordinarily fiendish ability to trick us into believing that all our unevolved thoughts, words and actions are justified and righteous. This is what causes war, abuse, neglect and all conflict in the world. Everyday the daily newspapers serve as a witness to the terrible things that people do to one another throughout the world. But, what's most frightening is that many, if not most, of these people firmly believe that they're doing the *right* thing – when they perform obvious injustices upon others. They sincerely believe that the killing, torture, abuse and injustice are justified, necessary and . . . right.

Recognize that ego, to greater or lesser degree, lurks in the shadow aspect of every personality on the planet. So, each of us has identical responsibility. Each of us can evolve – but only if we learn how to pull the plug on the egoic aspect of the personality. We short-circuit the ego's power when we focus upon the guidance of the infinitely wise soul. This requires **moment-by-moment awareness** – as the egoic shadow aspect of the personality always prefers to run amuck –

and ever shall do so – unless kept in line from one moment to the next; conquer (bypass) the monkeymind by focusing on soul, rather than ego. When ego does react, recognize and release egoic reactivity. Emotional release work and other vertical (soul-aligned) activities help to foster alignment of the personality. More will be discussed on this later.

Circumstance is not the cause of suffering – rather, the egoic aspect of the personality (ego) is the cause of all suffering. **The ego does not focus upon the present moment. It focuses only upon (so-called) past and (so-called) future.** Ego does not live in the present moment. Ego does not accept the present moment. Rather it looks back to false memory (biased and unreliable perception) of (so-called) past, and imagination (which is also biased and unreliable perception) of (so-called) future. Ego rejects the present moment. It does not accept the present nature of all things. *Non-acceptance by the ego is the cause of all pain.* Always. More will be discussed on this later.

THE TWO GREAT CHALLENGES (OF PERSONAL EVOLUTION): The soul's guidance to personality takes the form of intuition, synchronicity, dreams . . . and miracles. These forms of guidance are observed more frequently and with greater clarity when we transcend the unevolved, unaligned personality. So, *the first great challenge of our evolution is to understand, recognize and release the tentacles of the egoic unaligned personality. The second great challenge is to learn how to gain soul-focus (vertical alignment) in every moment – as this innately bypasses and dissipates the power of the unaligned personality (ego) – and hooks you up to an innate "stream of consciousness."* It's a "catch-22" situation. Focus on egoic thoughts begets more egoic thoughts. Focus on soul bypasses egoic thoughts – and opens a gateway to the soul's wisdom and "consciousness" – which enhances innate alignment and understanding. This serves to align our personality and material life with who we truly are at the core. So, focus on the soul by practicing soul-aligned (vertical) activity (described later in this text).

THE SOUL: In contrast to the personality, the soul is the aspect of self that seems *inspired by something larger than the sum of who we are.* Infinitely larger. Soul is the home of profoundly innovative ideas and creations that not atypically are judged by novice and expert alike as nothing less than "genius." Yet, soul is also home to subtlest, quietest, deepest truth. Soul is the womb of works as monumental as the inspired mathematics of Einstein, the music of Mozart, the art and science of Michelangelo, the prose of Shakespeare, and the kinesthetic prowess of Baryshnikov. Access to soul is how we find the subtle inkling of truth in the face of seemingly overwhelming uncertainty and doubt. Soul accesses the light that leads us out of darkness. Soul never fails us in the long-run. In contrast, ego always lets us down in the long-run.

SOUL IS THE GATEWAY FOR DIRECT CONNECTION TO CONSCIOUSNESS. Soul is the doorway to consciousness and eternal guidance. The soul is eternally plugged-in to consciousness and higher guidance. An ancient, esoteric group of Tibetans believed that human beings possess a primary energy system that runs vertically through the center of the body, connecting infinitely upward (to Heaven) and downward (to Earth). In essence, they believed that the human body serves as an electrical conduit which connects Heaven to Earth – via the body. They call this channel of energy the Antahkarana. They believe that the strength, vitality and linearity ("straight-ness") of the flow of this infinite channel defines our inner landscape. More aptly, they believe that this river IS our inner landscape (in its totality).

* * *

ANCILLARY CONCEPT

Ancient esotericists believed that the soul is a distinct energetic unit, and that the soul, known in some circles as the Soul Star, resides directly above the crown of the head (vertically aligned approximately twelve inches above the crown, in the auric field (a/k/a Aura) – in a position described as the Eighth Chakra.

* * *

This technical information is unimportant and resides outside the scope of this discussion. What matters is to be aware that the soul's connection to consciousness is always there. It is eternal. The soul never sleeps. It is always plugged-in to consciousness. The degree of our consciousness dictates the degree to which we are able to hear the soul's voice and guidance.

THE SOUL'S VOICE – THE VOICE OF TRUTH – TAKES THE FORM OF INTUITION, DREAMS, SYNCHRONICITY . . . AND MIRACLES. At times, truth can be subtle – as though a whisper. Barely audible, faintly detectable . . . yet profound. In other instances, truth can be abrupt and intense – like a jackhammer. Truth comes in many tones and forms.

> *"Bad information in*
> *Bad information out"*
>
> — Anonymous

Each of us can access truth – but first we must choose to receive truth. Like a computer, unless we receive correct information, we cannot calculate a correct outcome. If we receive tainted information, information that has been filtered through the selfish and near-sighted vision of the ego aspect of the personality, then our interpretation and decision-making based upon the data will be near-sighted – rendering a short-term non-solution to a long-term issue. The result is an uninformed decision that does not serve anyone's long-term best interest.

The soul speaks to us through four primary vehicles. *Internally* we are guided by the soul's subtle or not-so-subtle voices of intuition and dreams. *Externally* the soul guides us via synchronicity . . . and miracles.

INTUITION: We can sense truth. Sometimes it's simply a "gut feeling" about something. This is intuition. A quiet knowing that comes from deep within. A knowing that is always there – yet we cannot always access this inner voice, due to the distracted mind that at times, perhaps even most of the time, is unable to quiet itself sufficiently to allow audibility of the inner voice of truth – the voice of the soul. Certainly you've had a gut feeling about something in the past. Did you listen to the voice? Did it guide you appropriately? Or did you ignore its guidance? If so, as we so often do, did you notice in retrospect that the decision ended up leading you to another tough lesson, rather than a desired outcome?

We can influence whether or not we hear the inner voice of intuition. If we can still (bypass) the restless egoic aspect of personality, we can hear the inner voice of truth. Tools of sacred (inner) geometry help us bypass the ego, which opens us to the voice of intuition. These tools are discussed later in this text.

Intuition is a barometer that indicates the degree of our evolution. The more frequent the sense of intuition, the closer to the soul.

DREAMS: Dreams are another apparatus by which the soul guides us to higher ground. Much literature has been written regarding dreams and dream analysis. The sheer volume of text on the topic suggests that dream interpretation is a bit tricky. However, one simple truth is evident – the greater the clarity of the inner landscape, the greater the clarity of the guidance presented in dreams. A clean inner landscape (energetic template) renders direct guidance that is concise and clear – easy to interpret. In contrast, a stagnant, energetically-cluttered (*low vibration*) inner template results in convoluted dreams which are very difficult to interpret with any degree of confidence and accuracy. In these types of dreams you may receive bits and pieces of useful information, not atypically presented in the form of symbology, but the overall picture is unclear.

We *influence the nature of our dreams.* *First, clear up the inner landscape – including stagnant emotions and thought. Second, learn how to directly connect to the soul. Then, become a source of clear and concise guidance and information to rely upon.*

Conversely, enhanced clarity, conciseness, and on-pointedness of dreams indicate that the inner landscape is becoming more clear and thereby a more efficient conduit for the guidance of the soul.

SYNCHRONICITY: Unlike intuition and dreams – internal messages from the soul – synchronicity is a powerful *external* mechanism by which the soul guides those who recognize subtle (or not-so-subtle) external messages as a form of guidance. Synchronicity is disguised as sheer coincidence – a meaningless and inadvertent twist of fate. For this reason, the vast majority of people tend to ignore these profound road signs, as they do not recognize these signs as divine guidance. However, synchronicity is anything but coincidence.

Synchronicity is unexpected external guidance that piques our curiosity due to its unusual timing or uncanny message that somehow ties in to a current life situation. Sometimes it may feel like déjà vu – as though you've experienced something before, or as though you've already known something. It may simply remind you of something – a person, a place, an object, an event. It may simply affirm something that you already know. But, whatever the case, synchronicity provides a clue – a subtle or not-so-subtle hint regarding which path to take.

We indirectly create synchronicity. The more clear our inner landscape, the more our egoic personality is held at bay, the greater the frequency of synchronicity, and the greater our ability to recognize synchronous messages.

Conversely, the greater the frequency of synchronous events, the closer we are to the guidance of the soul.

MIRACLES: Hmmm . . . What can I say about miracles that you don't already know? Likely nothing. So, I will spare you from mere restatement of the obvious. Yet, do you realize that we create (cocreate) miracles? Unlikely as this may seem – *we create miracles.* Or, more precisely, we create the possibility for miracles to occur. How?

Miracles are external signs (exceptionally profound signs, indeed!) transmitted by natural order (a/k/a highest inspiration, the Infinite) via the soul. Although witnesses of miracles through the millennia have marveled at the miraculous deeds that seemed impossible to accomplish – the greater function of miracles regards inception of faith. "Except ye see signs and wonders, ye will not believe" (John 4:48). Faith that something greater than the sum of whom we are, is at play. Faith that goodness, for the sake of goodness, is not merely innately rewarded, but may also be materially rewarded (where aligned with natural order). Faith that natural order (highest inspiration, the Infinite) will take care of us – but only if we ask (through our intention, words and/or actions).

We create the possibility for miracles to occur by cleaning our inner landscape, and by tapping the soul. Then, when aligned with the will of natural order, miracles can occur.

Soul guidance in the form of intuition, dreams and synchronicity primarily guides us to higher ground in a material and etheric sense, and secondarily guide us to a growing sense of faith. Miracles do just the opposite – due to their extraordinary spontaneity and the scope of their exceptional action. The primary objective of miracles is to inspire faith. Secondarily, miracles guide us to higher ground in a material and etheric sense.

IF THE VOICE OF THE SOUL IS ALWAYS AVAILABLE, WHY DON'T WE ALWAYS HEAR AND CLEARLY DISCERN THE SOUL'S VOICE?

The voice of the soul is always available to us. The soul is always connected to truth. The soul is always willing to share its wisdom. But, the unaligned personality, the ego-driven aspect of the personality, blocks our innate ability to hear the soul's voice.

So, the trick is to **remain focused** upon the soul-aligned aspect of personality, rather than focus upon the unaligned, egoic aspect of personality. *This is simple in theory – yet challenging in practice.*

> *"All that you focus upon*
> *In the moment*
> *Is all that you are."*
>
> — Taoist Philosophy

The Taoists believe that this moment is all that exists. And this moment. And this moment. They believe that life is simply a series of moments. A sequence of snapshots. They do not label the past as "yesterday", nor the future as "tomorrow." Nor even the present day as "today." Rather, they keep it simple. They whittle all of life down to this moment. They learn to maintain a disciplined focus upon this moment. Then, this moment. And then, this moment. Why is this helpful? Because focus in the moment is a powerful way to bypass the scattered meanderings of the monkeymind – the unaligned, egoic aspect of the personality.

Present moment focus is facilitated by focus upon physical expression of the breath – especially focus upon the rise and fall of the lower abdomen. This form of body-centered breathwork (Abdominal Breathing) is theoretically simple, yet challenging – as this is a continual, *eternal*, moment-to-moment exercise. Body-centered breathwork has been practiced through the millennia on virtually every continent – to facilitate focus upon the present moment. Abdominal Breathing is an example of a method that inspires our natural inner geometry to align the energy of the bodymind with the vertical alignment of the soul. This discipline taps the wisdom of the soul – and instills presence.

Presence is the state of being that automatically instills connection to soul. Presence is a choice we make in each moment. It is binary. We are either present or not. There is no in-between.

Focus upon the present moment. Use methods that facilitate alignment with natural inner geometry. Vertically align with the energy of the soul. Live parallel to the soul. Only then can we hear the voice of the soul in every moment. Only then can we realize who we truly are, and identify and live our core life purpose and life service.

Unless we maintain mindfulness – unless we maintain focus upon the present moment, the voice of the soul is distant and relatively inaccessible. Without hearing this voice, it is improbable to live fully.

Although soul can guide us to higher ground, it cannot carry us there. For soul is focused upon our spiritual growth and evolution. Soul indirectly focuses upon the material world, but does not directly affect materiality. **To accomplish material feats, the soul calls upon the personality – for personality is Project Manager / Foreperson of material accomplishment. Soul is the Architect of our journey. But soul needs personality, the Project Manager / Foreperson to get the job done in the material world.** Presence connects us to the wisdom of the soul. And vice-versa. The mission of the soul is to help us to evolve – i.e., to help us master life lessons that are fundamental to each of us. To facilitate our inner evolution, the soul beckons us to master expression of love (and creativity) *in the world*. The extent of our expression of love (and creativity) in the world is a barometer of our inner landscape – our (inner) evolution. And, such outward expression begets further evolution. The soul cannot accomplish tasks in the material world on its own. It needs the help of the personality, its computer, to do so. **This is why it is so important for us to tame the reactive nature of the unevolved, egoic aspect of personality – so we can maintain soul-focus in every moment.**

Personality's focus regards our outer, material journey. In contrast, the soul's perspective, reach and scope focus primarily upon our inner journey. Of course, our inner and outer journeys influence one another. They are parallel universes that are dependent upon one another. We cannot grow internally without outer experience. We cannot evolve in the outer world without first evolving our inner journey. **Soul influences our experience in the outer world, which transpires as a direct reflection (mirror image) of the degree of our overall inner evolution.** Soul's responsibility is our progressive inner evolution (i.e., mastery of life lessons).

Consider the choice of monks to live, work and play in isolated monasteries. Their (presumed) intention is to accelerate their spiritual journey through non-distracted meditation, study, and communion with natural order, nature and others of like-mind and like-intention. They choose to live in an environment that minimizes outer distraction – to inspire and support inner transformation. Yet, could it be that lack of interaction in the uncontrolled material world – of dualistic highs, lows and random external triggering – may actually slow the process of evolution (for some individuals)? Why might this be?

My greatest teacher (an anonymous, profound meditator) presents two answers regarding the profound question of where the most appropriate forum for self-evolution might be. First, he said that one needn't "go to the Himalayas to grow spiritually." Second he stated, "If you can attain a state of self-awareness here [in Hollywood, California], then you can attain it anywhere." In other words, he teaches that not only is it not necessary to visit an isolated quiet sanctuary to attain self-awareness, in fact this might be counter-productive (for some of us). He advocates that a life spent engaged in the seeming chaos and frequent annoyances of the everyday world heighten the need to learn how to tame unbridled emotional reactivity and stagnant (non-accepting, judgmental) thoughts – which arise in response to these annoyances ("triggers"). He views annoyances as a gift, as they force us to learn how to deal with the emotional reactivity and negative thought patterns that arise in response to these annoyances. "Our greatest nemesis is our greatest teacher" – as she is the most powerful trigger of emotional and mental reactivity . . . and subsequent self-learning and healing.

Overall, could it be that the most appropriate forum in which to gain self-awareness (evolution), what the Taoists call the "Middle Way" – is the path of moderation? Could it be that a balance of exposure to both a controlled meditative environment (a virtual monastery) on occasion, and daily exposure to an uncontrolled environment (i.e., daily living) – to expose oneself to daily doses of triggering – is an effective mix to foster personal evolution?

Of course, the optimal path to self-awareness varies for every person. The choice to live in a monastery to further one's spiritual evolution may be an appropriate decision for one person, but not for another person. The choice to live in a monastery may be appropriate at a specific stage in one's life, but not for a different time in life. Many factors influence the question of how to best gain self-awareness. One such factor regards a person's specific stage of personal development. For example, if a person is easily distracted, or if an individual has never experienced a sense of profound stillness, it may be appropriate for her to visit a monastery (real or virtual) to jump-start the path toward serenity and meditation. This is especially helpful as **it is easiest to meditate once we have a reference point for the experience of meditation** (i.e., firsthand knowledge of the feeling of a true meditative experience). However, once a person has experienced the profound stillness possible through meditation, then it may be that routine living "in the world" is an effective path – to bolster the ability to deal with emotional and mental reactivity triggered by life's annoyances.

For instance, while living in Chicago I notice that many of the more experienced healers that I meet spend at least a couple of months, if not years, living in quasi-monastic centers (frequently in California). Thereafter they returned to urban centers (in Chicago and other cities and towns) to set-up professional practice and continue their personal journey. This seems consistent with my path. As much as I enjoyed living in a gorgeous, quasi-monastic setting, I now enjoy living in downtown Chicago. Everyday I learn lessons that I might not have been exposed to had I remained in a remote environment. Trust that you are exactly where you need to be in the moment – to learn and master whatever it is that you're meant to learn.

In summation, the soul cannot effectively complete its mission in the world without help from the aligned personality. Living in the everyday world helps us sculpt the personality into alignment with soul, if we choose to learn from each lesson presented.

As an example of personality and soul working together as a team, the soul guides the aligned personality to recognize, understand, and eventually express core life purpose and life service. On a grand scale, this helps us to evolve spiritually. The mechanism is straightforward. The soul is eternally aware of the truth of who we are on all levels – for the soul *is* the true self. The soul is eternally aware of our *core life purpose – how we "give" to ourselves* (self-focused, solo activity that brings us profound inner joy and vitality based upon inner passion for core creativity – which involves no one else; this activity involves creation of music, visual art or dance/movement). And, the soul is eternally aware of our *core life service (activity that "gives" to others* in a profound, aligned way). Yet, **soul cannot express (i.e., perform) life purpose and life service in the world without the help of the soul-aligned personality.** The soul may know what our life purpose and service are – but it cannot perform them in the world as soul is directly focused on our inner journey and only *indirectly* focused upon our material world experience. It is the role of personality to directly focus upon, and physically manifest, our material journey – in accordance to the guidance of the soul.

UNINSPIRED THOUGHT VERSUS INSPIRED THOUGHT.

"Uninspired thought" refers to mental images, ideas, interpretations, and revelations that lack sacred (profound) foundation. The underpinning of these thoughts is fueled by the ego's limited negative perspective (of non-acceptance and judgment). The trickery of the ego attempts to lead us to believe that these thoughts *are* inspired and based in highest creativity and truth.

In contrast, inspired thought is filtered-down via the soul. Inspired thought is sourced by an intangible, eternal, infinitely creative, omniscient, omnipresent force (Highest Inspiration, Natural Order, Light, God, etc.) Inspired thought is aligned with the truth of who we are at the core. Always. Inspired thought is based in universal truth and expresses truth. Always. Inspired thought is aware of what is best for us – in the long-run. Always. Inspired thoughts supersede and guide the mechanical steps required for profound creation.

Inspired thought will never let us down. Or anyone else. Uninspired thought will let us down every time. Perhaps not at first, but later on down the road.

> *"Careful what you wish for*
> *For you just might receive it."*
>
> — Anonymous

Ego, the source of uninspired thought, hasn't a clue as to who we truly are. Ego's horizon of vision is limited. Ego and its uninspired thoughts seek immediate gratification. Ego does not consider the long-term consequences of words and actions. ***Uninspired thoughts typically desire objects, people, events and outcomes that do not serve us in the long-run.*** The solutions posed by ego and uninspired thought are like the proverbial finger placed in the initial tiny hole in a dam. It may be enough to stop seepage of water for a moment or two. But, the build-up of water behind the dam will soon overcome the near-sighted solution put forth by the ego. Ego presents meager solutions (like band-aids) to gaping problems as it does not see complete truth – it cannot see the enormity and long-term consequences associated with a given scenario. All it sees is the immediate trickle of water down an embankment – not the coming floodwaters. And, given its limited, narrow field of vision which sees the totality of the threat as nothing more than the trickle of water from a tiny hole, ego sincerely believes that one finger in the dike is the appropriate solution. So ego tries to trick us into believing this. This is the danger of ego – its inability to see the complete picture – combined with its expert ability to trick us into believing that it knows the best answer. For this reason, careful what you wish for – for if the desire is based in ego it will serve you only in the short-run (and may exacerbate the long-term scenario).

Ponder the following question. *Do you **always** make appropriate decisions – that serve the highest good for all involved parties?* If you're a typical human, most certainly you do not. And hopefully you're sufficiently self-aware to realize that you don't always make proper decisions. **The reason we make inappropriate decisions is that all-too-often we unknowingly call upon the personality (lower mind / ego mind) to guide our decisions.** The ego hasn't a clue as to who we truly are. The ego cannot discern what is best for us and all others in the long-run. **The ego and uninspired thought have limited fields of vision – and can only pose band-aid answers** that cause the decision-making process to consider only a very narrow (and typically selfish) band of focus, and short-term timeline.

The uninspired personality's thoughts lack creativity of profound (sacred) dimension. Uninspired thoughts (sometimes referred to as "unconscious" thoughts) can adequately direct non-creative processes, such as driving a car, executing 90 percent of all worldly tasks (to a standard of adequacy), and even posing what may seem like somewhat creative solutions to mundane problems. For example, uninspired thought may propose a new way to unclog a bathtub, hang a painting, drive a new way to work to avoid traffic, learn a new software program, ride a motorcycle, etc. But these uninspired accomplishments pale in comparison to the works of inspired thought. Such as the divinely-inspired masterpieces that include Mozart's symphonies (including those written as a child), Michelangelo's David, Baryshnikov's dance, Shakespeare's works, Pele's soccer dominance, and Michael Jordan's basketball mastery. The uninspired personality's thoughts lack originality and capacity of sacred dimension. In contrast, divinely-inspired thoughts are selfless, patient, tolerant, compassionate, and timeless. Inspired (aligned) mind seeks long-term gratification. Higher mind accesses the sacred – including what some philosophers describe as the Stream of Consciousness – an etheric river of truth. The inspired aspect of the personality (higher mind) is receptive to intuition, dreams, synchronicity and miracles accessed by the soul. The uninspired aspect of personality is not receptive to soul guidance.

THOUGHTS ARE BINARY. THEY EITHER SUPPORT OR BLOCK TRUTH. There is no in-between. Uninspired thoughts, thoughts inspired by the ego-driven aspect of the personality, block truth. Inspired thoughts, guided by the eternal wisdom of the soul, support flow of the river of truth. **So, we have a choice to make. In each moment we must decide whether to focus upon inspired thought (soul-aligned, soul-guided thought) or uninspired (ego-aligned) thought.** Should we choose not to consciously make this decision in each moment, the odds are that ego-driven thoughts will guide us, and our decision-making process, by default. We must ask ourselves the following questions. What do we want? Do we want to continue to make the same repetitive mistakes? Do we want to remain relatively unaware of our mission in life – our soul's great purpose and service? Do we prefer to remain oblivious to subtle aspects of our true path and nature? Are we open to the possibility that ancient technology (sacred geometric activities and supplements) and philosophy (soul-alignment via internal energetic verticality), which have withstood the test of time, may actually be helpful?

THE ONLY THING WE CAN CONTROL IN THIS LIFE IS EACH THOUGHT IN EACH MOMENT. We cannot control other people's thoughts, words, or actions. We cannot control objects, events or outcomes. We cannot control what will occur tomorrow. Yet, **we can control our thoughts in each moment. Why is this a valuable exercise? Because our thoughts create our inner landscape (energetic template). And our inner energetic template shapes our outer experience in the material world. So,** *paradoxically, although we cannot control other people, objects, events or outcomes – we can indirectly yet effectively influence people, objects, events and outcomes.* This is a great paradox and a secret key to effective manifestation. More will be revealed on this later.

THOUGHT TRIGGERS EMOTION. EMOTION IS THE BODY'S REACTION TO THOUGHT. Why is it important to understand how emotions work? Because unhealthy (reactive) emotions can block access to guidance by the soul – and the truth of whom we are. For example, have you ever been so consumed by anger – even if for just a minute or two – that you had trouble focusing on the task at hand, not to mention focusing on profound truth? The point is that it's difficult, if not impossible, to clearly hear your inner voice (intuition) when in the throes of "unhealthy" emotion – be it immense and loitering anger, sadness, worry and/or fear. Unhealthy emotions also block access to synchronicity, dreams . . . and miracles.

It is important to understand the nature of emotion – so we can effectively, efficiently and immediately *process* unhealthy emotion (*i.e., reveal, feel and release emotion*) to heal potential blockages to guidance by the soul.

Emotions are a natural and essential aspect of who we are. Emotions are the body's natural and essential reaction to the mind's thoughts. Yet, so many of us seem to be soooooooo afraid of emotions – afraid both to feel and express emotion. Afraid to feel and express profound fear, sadness, worry and anger. In this contemporary society, many of us are taught that it is not gentile to express anger. Nor to complain. Nor to be afraid – as action heroes in movies are depicted as never experiencing fear. Thus, we bury sadness, anger, fear and worry. These emotions are shoved under the rug to the subconscious basement of the mind. There, although seemingly dormant at surface, they brew and gain even greater intensity. From time to time, we feel anger, and sadness, fear and worry bubble up from beneath the surface. Sometimes we haven't a clue as to why we feel what we feel. At other times it may be obvious that something triggered us to experience specific emotions. At times our response may be a bit excessive – a bit "over-dramatic" relative to the degree of (external) annoyance. In energy work sessions facilitated over a period of seven years, I observed that some people try to hide from feeling altogether – as they associate pain and suffering with *feeling*, which begets further pain and suffering; recall that only the egoic aspect of personality experiences pain and suffering – the aligned personality and soul do not experience pain and suffering.

Interestingly, both contemporary Western psychologists and ancient Eastern (holistic) philosophers recognize that buried emotion tends to attract even more turbulence into one's life. How is this possible?

Western psychology recognizes that buried emotion becomes like a filter over our eyes and other senses, and skews our view and interpretation of everything external to us (people, objects, events and outcomes). We don't see things as they are and, rather, we transfer ("project") our buried emotional landscape onto situations, needlessly.

Eastern psychology believes that buried emotion magnetically attracts further emotional turbulence. The mechanism is a bit esoteric – yet simple in theory, if you can accept the underpinnings of this seemingly obscure paradigm. The fundamental assumptions of this Eastern theory are:

1)   Everything is comprised of energy.
2)   Energy attracts similar energy.

Energy of buried emotions attracts situations that cause more of the same type of emotions to be experienced. In other words, buried emotion begets more of the same emotion. For example, suppose that you were very angry about a situation that occurred in your life, but you didn't express all the anger you felt (in an appropriate manner). You buried the remaining anger. Easterners believe that the anger buried deep inside must be released. But, in this example you did not choose to feel and subsequently release the anger. Rather you chose to bury the anger. So, Easterners believe the only way that you will heal (i.e., unbury and release the anger) is to throw additional triggers of anger at you! In essence, they believe that a healing crisis is the only way that you will completely heal your *relationship* with anger. **A healing crisis involves being so overwhelmed by pain and suffering that we no longer choose to avoid dealing with an uncomfortable condition – in this case emotional suffering. Rather, the pain and suffering motivate us to find a way to heal.** So, in this example, for you to heal your relationship with anger – rather than bury more anger, your buried anger serves as a magnet to attract so much more anger (in reaction to externalities) so that you can no longer bury the anger. You have to deal with it. You are forced to finally feel the anger – no matter how much you dislike the feeling. And you are forced to find a way to heal the anger – only because you are so very uncomfortable dealing with the anger. So, you eventually learn how to feel and release the anger in a healthy manner (Anger Release Work). More will be covered on this later. Suffice it to say that any buried (i.e., unprocessed, unreleased) emotion acts like a magnet to attract more of the same emotion – to overwhelm you to such extent that you can no longer hide from the emotion, so you actively pursue healing your relationship with that specific emotion. The energy of the buried emotion attracts more of the same energy. Thus it is said that "like begets like." This certainly holds true for unresolved emotion. Unresolved emotion begets more of the same emotion (to force a healing crisis – which forces you to heal).

Many of us try to hide from our emotions. Certainly none of us *enjoy* feeling anger, sadness, worry and sorrow. We prefer not to experience any "negative" (from ego's judgmental perspective) emotions. We prefer to simply feel peaceful, serene, harmonious, and happy. We prefer to avoid the distraction of unpleasant emotions. This is one of a plethora of valid reasons why people enter monasteries . . . to avoid the distractive annoyances (emotional triggers) of the external world. And yet, there is so much value to learning how to deal with emotional triggers – for this is where profound healing can occur. Healing which can liberate us from the limitations and sufferings of the ego-driven personality. This serves to ultimately help us align with the soul – and our truth, including our core life purpose and life service, in every moment.

Your greatest nemesis
Is your greatest teacher
For she who spotlights
The undisciplined aspect of your mind
Helps you
To master yourself

It is both essential and masterful to learn the art of emotional release. This is a method by which to quickly gain momentum for soul-aligned success. Once you achieve a degree of mastery of the emotions and emotional release, you may begin to sense the ebb and flow of daily energy – which fluctuates every hour, by design (to help trigger as-yet unresolved emotions). You may see through the reasons underlying the external triggers of daily life – and will learn to thank your greatest nemesis (for it is she who brings greatest self-healing and transformation, by triggering unresolved emotions). You may ultimately attain and maintain inner peace, serenity, understanding, and harmony – even in the face of uncertainty and seeming external chaos. Yet, until then . . . unfortunately there is little choice regarding the matter of the emotions. Your choices are either to learn how to completely feel and release emotions – or to bury the emotions in the shadows of the subconscious mind, and beget greater turbulence in future moments, which serves to attract even greater turbulence thereafter. Again and again and again (et al). Until you are inspired by repetitive discomfort to finally learn how to feel and release emotional reactivity. A gift.

CONCEPTION OF AN EMOTION, THE BODY'S RESPONSE TO MIND'S THOUGHT, IS A THREE-STEP PROCESS. *To release emotion, engage this process – in reverse.* Why is it important to understand the mechanism underlying how an emotion is created and stored? So that we can understand how to efficiently release "unhealthy" emotion – and so release (egoic) resistance to soul-guidance.

Recall that emotion is the body's response to mental thought. Conception of an emotion is a three-step process. First, an external event occurs. As an example, suppose that lightning strikes a nearby tree. Second, your mind instantly creates a thought in response to the lightning – such as "yikes – what if the tree falls and hits me or others?" In this example, the lightning is a "mental trigger", since the lightning served to trigger a reaction by the mind. Third, the thought created in the mind, a fearful thought in this example, stimulates a reaction by the endocrine system. The endocrine (hormone) system's job is to *immediately transcribe and transmit* the mind's message, where appropriate, to the body (specific receptor sites on a corresponding internal organ) – to prepare the body for whatever action might be appropriate for a given circumstance. In this example, the falling tree evokes a "fight or flight" reaction by the body, by causing specific hormones to enter the bloodstream and bind to receptor sites in the kidneys (where "fear potential" is stored in biochemical form).

In summary, an external event (mental/emotional trigger) causes the brain to experience a mental (electrical) response (a sequence of brainwave spikes if viewed ala an EEG, Electroencephalograph machine). Brainwaves in the form of electrical impulses then tell the endocrine glands to transcribe the electrical brain patterns, the mental reaction, into a specific corresponding biochemical sequence that is then carried via the blood stream to specific receptor sites on one or more internal organs. In this way, the body is alerted and readied for action regarding an imminent event. Fear is stored in the kidneys; anger is stored in the liver – consider the stereotypical "angry" drunk – both anger and alcohol are processed by the liver; worry is stored in the pancreas, spleen and stomach; and sadness and sorrow are stored in the lungs – consider the widely-held observation that the process of grief not atypically causes respiratory dysfunction including bronchitis and pneumonia – as sadness and sorrow are released from the lungs – actually a good thing!

Again, the reason it is important to understand how an emotion is conceived is so that we can engage the process in reverse, to most effectively and efficiently release "unhealthy" emotion. The point is that we must first approach the body to release stagnant emotions (as emotion is the body's response to thought). Then we analyze and shift the "negative" thought patterns that caused the sequence of conception of the unhealthy emotion.

THE BODYMIND: The endocrine system serves as an intermediary between mind and body, and functionally unifies mind and body. For this reason, Eastern philosophy considers the body and mind to be a single unit, the "bodymind." Mind influences body – and vice-versa.

EMOTIONS ARE EITHER FLOWING (HEALTHY) OR BLOCKED (UNHEALTHY). Eastern philosophy views health and vitality as a river (of energy). A river with unimpeded flow is healthy. A river with blocked or restricted flow is unhealthy. Healthy, flowing emotions support our inner landscape and aligned material success. Healthy emotions help us access guidance by the soul (via intuition, synchronicity, dreams . . . and miracles). And, healthy emotions promote physical health. In contrast, unhealthy emotions block access to the wisdom of the soul, deteriorate and clutter our inner landscape, block aligned material success, and impair physical health.

HEALTHY EMOTIONS ARE INSPIRED BY POSITIVE THOUGHTS. Mere restatement of the obvious, eh? Certainly the contemporary adage "don't worry – be happy!" is easier said than done . . . until we learn to focus in the present moment.

UNHEALTHY EMOTION IS CAUSED BY UNINSPIRED THOUGHTS, BIRTHED IN THE UNALIGNED PERSONALITY. The thoughts of the unaligned personality (ego) are precursors to "unhealthy" (low vibration) emotions, which are stored in the internal organs. To release these emotions and prevent recurrence, first release an emotion from the body, then release (re-pattern) the unaligned brainwave pattern from the egoic aspect of the personality/mind.

Chapter Two

THE NATURE
OF
ENERGY

Everything is made of energy.
Contemporary scientists
And ancient meditators agree.
Heaven. Earth. Sky. Sea.
Body. Mind.
You. Me. Us. Them.
Thought. Emotion.
So-called Past. So-called Future.
All connected
To the Here and Now
On the Wings of Breath
Intention
Word
Action

EVERYTHING IS MADE OF ENERGY – INCLUDING THOUGHT, EMOTION, PHYSICAL HEALTH, SUCCESS, ETC. The chair you sit upon. The floor beneath the chair. The Earth beneath the floor. The ceiling above you. The roof above the ceiling. The sky above the roof. The Heaven above sky. And all in between. All that is tangible. All that is intangible. The air you breathe. All you create. All creation. All people. All objects. All events. Every thought you have ever entertained or may entertain. Love, hate, brilliance, dullness, creativity, limitation. Every emotion that you have experienced or may experience. Joy, anger, sadness, worry, fear, all experiences, facts and illusions you have known and ever shall know. In sum, everything that has ever existed, exists, or that shall ever exist in the physical, mental, emotional and spiritual aspects of being is comprised of energy.

A PARTICLE OF ENERGY CAN NEITHER BE CREATED NOR DESTROYED. The First Law of Thermodynamics (Physics 101) states that a particle of energy can be neither created nor destroyed. Energy is a pre-existing condition. A pre-existing state of the universe. Energy simply is. Everything is comprised of energy. Always was. And ever shall be.

A GROUPING OF ENERGY PARTICLES TRAVELS IN THE FORM OF A WAVE. Energy particles either attract or repel one another. Essentially, this is a binary condition (ignoring transitory conditions and other anomalies of neutrality). For practical purposes, there is no in-between. Western quantum physicists long ago observed that *an electron exhibits a dual personality that exhibits the dualistic characteristics of both a particle and wave.* Certain energy particles attract one another and travel together in groups. A grouping of energetic particles may exhibit movement described as a wave of energy – an energetic waveform.

ALL ENERGY PARTICLES (AND WAVEFORMS) AFFECT ONE ANOTHER. Energy particles and waveforms attract and repel one another. Energy particles that repel one another travel separately – yet still influence the path of one another. As an example of repulsion, what happens if you place oil and vinegar together in a bowl? The oil and vinegar separate – as their charges repel one another. They remain separate yet affect the path of one another. This is common knowledge.

> *"A hummingbird flaps its wings in Japan*
> *[And] a hurricane occurs in the Azores."*
>
> — Anonymous

The tiniest energetic wave formed in Asia affects energy in Africa – and potentially to a great degree. How is it possible that an Asian hummingbird's activity can influence an event in a location as distant as Africa? And, especially an event of such great magnitude? The answer is that energy affects <u>all</u> energy. Nothing occurs in a vacuum. Literally, everything is interconnected – by energy – as everything is energy.

As a trite example, consider the fact that air is energy. Air envelopes everything on land – and thereby connects everything on land. Similarly, water envelopes everything in the oceans – and thusly all oceanic aquatic life is interconnected by water. Light fills the universe (including Earth, of course) and connects everything. Quantum physicists discovered that everything is made up of quantum particles – which are bits of light . . . light particles. Similarly, many ancient cultures postulated, thousands of years ago, that everything is made of light. Thus, modern scientists and ancient philosophers alike concluded that everything is made of light. Light particles not merely envelope everything – but permeate everything. Light particles inter-connect everything. Thought. Emotion. People. Objects. Events. Experiences. And all else. Light particles **are** everything. Everything is comprised of light particles.

The Asian Hummingbird's energetic activity plants an energetic seed that grows over (so-called) time and (so-called) space; time and space are illusory yet practical concepts when contemplating material world conditions. Through mechanisms that involve a multitude of causal energetic and meteorological factors, the hummingbird's activity inspires the birth of an African hurricane. As an abstract yet unlikely scenario, perhaps wind flow generated by the Hummingbird accelerated evaporation of nearby water droplets. The evaporated water rose toward sky, and somehow inspired other droplets to evaporate, which eventually joined the initial droplet to form a cloud, that inspired other clouds to form and join, and that these clouds, over the course of a journey of thousands of kilometers and weeks, eventually became the eye of a hurricane in the Azores. *The point is that even the slightest thought, word or action can cause great effect in the material world. Energy particles affect all other energy particles – regardless how distant.*

ALTHOUGH ENERGETIC WAVEFORMS EXPRESS THEMSELVES IN AN INFINITE ARRAY OF THREE-DIMENSIONAL SHAPES, CERTAIN SHAPES RECUR MOST FREQUENTLY IN NATURE. Vortices are spiraling waveforms that are frequently seen in all levels of nature – especially with regard to primordial, rudimentary aspects of nature. For example, the universe and galaxies are enormous spiraling vortices of stars, planets and intergalactic stuff. Similarly, galactic black holes are described as vortices. On a more local and subtle level, a fundamental element of human beings, namely DNA (deoxyribonucleic acid), the map of our genetic template, is a double-sided helix – a vortex that defines the blueprint of who we are. Both the "macro" – the universe – and the "micro" – the human body – developed from vortices.

Waveforms may travel in the form of spirals or may be linear. *The essence of human inner geometry is vertical – as aligned with the soul (via the Antahkarana).* **The physioneurological core of the human body, the spinal column, tangibly parallels the alignment of core,**

vertically-aligned energetic waveforms. Chiropractors and Osteopaths zealously believe that unimpeded energetic flow through the erect, healthy spine encourages health. Similarly, ancient philosophers believed that **unimpeded vertical energetic flow supports health, and that impeded vertical flow – tantamount to horizontal flow – blocks health.** *In addition to the tangible vertical spine, our inner geometry consists of intangible vertical (soul-aligned) energy meridians that pierce the core of the bodymind.*

ENERGETIC WAVEFORMS MAY BE RE-SHAPED (INFLUENCED). We can influence the shape of (re-shape) pre-existing waveform patterns. This is accomplished by introducing a new energetic force into a scenario; and/or adding to, decreasing from, or re-directing a pre-existing force in the scenario. For instance, let's re-examine the oil and vinegar example of repulsion. What happens if we add more of either substance (but not both) into the bowl? The result is a pattern of enhanced repulsion. Our activity transforms (influences) the shape of the oil-vinegar mixture in the bowl. We re-shape the waveforms of the oil and vinegar by influencing (adding) more of one of the ingredients. *The point – we can influence the pattern of waveforms. This is a vital piece of information with regard to transformation of all conditions – including our lives.*

WE EMIT ELECTROMAGNETIC WAVEFORMS AS THOUGH WE ARE A BELL. Strike a bell and its resonation rings out over great distance for a prolonged period of time. Similarly, the resonations of our inner energetic movements ring out over distance and for a considerable duration of time. The resonance of our inner landscape, our inner energetic template, rings out over infinite time and space – affecting everything in the universe. Like a bell, our inner resonance has greatest effect nearby, with progressively decreased effect upon anything distant. Nonetheless, our inner resonance does affect everything, even if only slightly, regardless how distant. Recall the example of the Asian hummingbird and the hurricane in the Azores. Our inner resonance rings out and re-shapes pre-existing waveforms throughout the universe. So, our inner resonance has the power to re-shape everything and anything within the universe.

THE LAW OF ATTRACTION AND HEALING CRISES: The Law of Attraction states that energy attracts like-energy. Why? To help us evolve. The Law of Attraction promotes healing crises – a fast-track to self-awareness, evolution and material success.

Energy begets like-energy.
Anger begets anger.
Sadness begets sadness.
Fear begets fear.
Joy begets joy.
Confusion begets confusion.

Negativity begets negativity.
Positivity begets positivity.
To teach us
About the unresolved aspects
Of ourselves.
To show us
The undisciplined aspects
Of the mind.
Sometimes we heal
Only when conditions and feelings
Become so overwhelmingly uncomfortable
That we have no choice
But to learn how to heal.
This shows the value of healing crises -
Conditions of overwhelming discomfort.
A great gift in the long-run.

The Law of Attraction
Attracts triggers
To inspire healing crises
To speed our self-awareness
Evolution
Material success
Happiness, Joy and Bliss.

The Law of Attraction draws people, objects and events to us that trigger the unevolved aspects of the unconscious (and conscious) mind to react – ultimately facilitating enhanced self-awareness. For this reason it is said that your greatest perceived nemesis is your greatest teacher – for it is she who reveals the undisciplined aspect of your mind – the unresolved aspects of the unconscious and conscious personality.

It is essential to release
Buried unconscious and conscious unresolved energies
To create a successful experience in the world.
Body-centered breath, sensory activity and external sensory-stimulating
supplements
Are a fast-track to release
Unresolved buried energies.

The Law of Attraction states that the unresolved unconscious and conscious aspects of our personalities act like magnets that attract lessons to help us heal our unresolved aspects. The props for these lessons are specific people, objects and events. These props serve to "trigger" us to feel (a/k/a unbury) previously buried unresolved thoughts, emotions and other energies. The specific people, objects and events attracted to us, by our electromagnetic emissions, cause (trigger) us to unbury core "stuff" that we've held deep inside for years. Just like a pimple – which can only heal if the purulent exudates (pus) beneath comes to surface – **we can resolve unconscious and conscious (buried) issues only by bringing the** *original feelings* **to surface. The triggers** *cause us to feel the same (original) feelings that we weren't ready to feel long ago* **– as they felt overwhelmingly uncomfortable at that time.** A healing crisis is an experience that causes us to feel the same overwhelming emotions and thoughts that were too difficult to process (feel) in the past. **Healing crises are promoted by the Law of Attraction – which draws triggers to us to help us unearth buried unresolved energies.** This serves to help us create lives we prefer – rather than create lives we most definitely shall not prefer – by default.

WE CONSCIOUSLY AND UNCONSCIOUSLY EMIT ELECTROMAGNETIC WAVEFORMS THAT PRECISELY MIRROR (MIMIC) THE QUALITY OF OUR INNER LANDSCAPE – INCLUDING THOUGHTS AND EMOTIONS – THAT INSTANTANEOUSLY TRAVEL THROUGHOUT THE WORLD (AND UNIVERSE). Our innermost thoughts, emotions, subconscious memories, and cellular memories affect the world around us. Again, like a bell, these conscious and unconscious aspects of our core ring out to the world and universe. They affect anything closest to us most profoundly – yet still affect all else. As esoteric as this may sound, this information has practical value. Be aware that our conscious and unconscious energies have the power to re-shape the world surrounding us.

One-third of the electromagnetic waveforms that we emit stem from our conscious thoughts and emotions. We must take responsibility for these thoughts and emotions. We must learn how to transform conscious thoughts and emotions – to create a life experience that we prefer. Otherwise we simply create a life experience by default – a life that mirrors unhealthy thoughts and emotions. For example, if we consciously experience frequent worry – we attract people, objects and events that cause us to worry even more than we already do. In other words, these triggers (the people, objects and events) cause us to feel so much worry that we eventually feel overwhelmed (healing crisis) – to such degree that we finally realize that we have no choice except to heal the emotion of worry (or continue to suffer).

Two-thirds of the electromagnetic waveforms that we emit stem from our unconscious aspect. Although it may seem unfair (if we ignore the concept of karma) to be responsible for subconscious "thought" (energetic) patterns that we are unaware of – be aware that subconscious thoughts profoundly affect the world surrounding us. Electromagnetic radiation mirroring unhealthy sub*conscious* energetic patterns – buried subconscious thoughts and emotions - attract triggers and lessons.

So . . . take responsibility! Facilitate resolution of unhealthy conscious thoughts and emotions by employing external sensory-stimulating supplements to promote alignment with the wisdom of the soul (verticality). Resolve unhealthy unconscious energetic patterns. This serves to minimize radiation of unhealthy electromagnetic energy into the world – which, again, creates "un-preferred" experiences by default. *Proactive self-awareness* helps us to create preferred life experiences and outcomes.

* * *

ANCILLARY CONCEPT

Karma

What causes subconscious electromagnetic patterns to arise deep within us? This is a profound question that has been pondered through the millennia. Why is it important to answer this seemingly esoteric and impractical question? So we gain prowess at creating our lives – our experience in the world. Otherwise we continue to create by default – attracting an outer experience that mirrors an unhealthy inner landscape (and subjects us to unpleasant, uncomfortable, nonpreferred people, objects, events, and experiences – repeatedly – until we master the lessons and resolve the unhealthy conscious patterns).

Ancient cultures believed that "you reap what you sow." They believed that the phenomenon of cause-and- effect is a driving force behind creation. Do good unto another, and receive good. Do bad unto another, and suffer unpleasant consequences. Not as punishment but, rather, to teach us an appropriate lesson. This is the theory of karma. Karma is energetic justice. Karma evens the score – hurt someone, and suffer the consequences yourself. Help someone, and be helped. Karma is a great teacher. It teaches the unaligned aspect of personality to align with soul by engaging in appropriate behavior, word and thought.

Certain philosophies profess that karmic debt, the remaining imbalance of unresolved lessons, comprises the bulk of the subconscious, unresolved, unhealthy aspect of the personality. It is this karmic debt that subconsciously attracts lessons that account for two-thirds of the electromagnetic radiation that we present to the world, which attracts (a/k/a creates) the reality we live and continue to manifest.

External sensory-stimulating supplements are an effective method by which to release karmic debt and unresolved subconscious energies from psyche'. You cannot shift karmic debt through intellect (alone).

*   *   *

THE QUALITY OF CONSCIOUS AND UNCONSCIOUS ELECTRO-MAGNETIC WAVEFORMS IS BINARY. They either support or hinder evolution and material success. A healthy river flows freely, without restriction. The water is clear, vital, life-supporting and life-sustaining. In contrast, the flow of an unhealthy river is blocked and relatively stagnant. The water may be murky, turbulent in certain places, or unmoving. Similar to a river, the inner energetic river may be free-flowing (healthy), or it may be blocked or restricted (unhealthy). The Law of Attraction causes a cloudy inner landscape to attract a cloudy material experience. A clear inner landscape attracts a clear life experience.

So, clear your inner channels. Use external sensory-stimulating supplements to facilitate release of unresolved energies, and to tap the brilliant wisdom of the soul.

* * *

ANCILLARY CONCEPT

Energy is binary
(Real or False)

Be forewarned that dealing with energy is a bit tricky. An experience may be truly energizing – feeding the soul; or an experience may bear merely the illusion of energy – feeding the ego, not soul. True energy renders true power. And feeds the soul – for soul is the home of core truth and true power. False (illusory) energy renders false power. False energy feeds the ego – for ego is the home of false power. So, energy is binary. It is either real or false (illusory). There is no in-between.

It is helpful to consider energy to be of two forms – either real or false (illusory). Real energy particles are, simply, particles of light. False, illusory energy, technically, is lack of light. However, for simplicity herein, false energy is defined as anything (other than light) that feeds the (perception of the) ego. False energy is anything, other than light, that the ego perceives as vitalizing.

For example, trees are a source of true energy. Trees vitalize anything within their proximity – providing not merely oxygen and water molecules as products of photosynthesis but, of equal importance, trees radiate light energy. So, trees are a source of access to true energy. The Taoists prescribe sitting next to a tree, and meditating with a tree (Tree Meditation in Qi Gong – pronounced "chee/gong"), to invigorate our inner energetic landscape. As a simple exercise, sit with your back to a tree for twenty minutes. Breathe. Do you notice a change in temperament?

In contrast, an example of a source of false energy is ego's dominance (bullying) over another person – regardless whether in the workplace or home. The bully feels a false sense of power (and control) in the moment while dominating another. Dominance over another is a source of false power. This type of power is not based in light, and thus is illusory. The ego perceives power surges based not from light, but from illusory sources of energy. These perceived surges are very short-lived. Then the ego seeks yet another short-term "fix."

* * *

SOURCES OF ENERGY. Western scientists and Eastern meditators agree that light particles (quantum particles) are the essence of energy. Light is the ultimate, and only, direct source of true energy. Energy may be accessed internally or externally.

HIERARCHY OF ACCESS TO ENERGY: A GREAT PARADOX

Paradox. n.
A statement that seems contrary to common sense, and yet may be true.

A timeless hint.
Highest energy is accessed
Not via the two human eyes
But through the inner eye.
So go within.

Anti-logical, esoteric, and impractical as it may seem, we must "go within" to access highest-quality energy. This facilitates attainment of self-awareness, which serves to reveal our core life purpose and life service. Try as we might, we do not find *highest*-quality energy by seeking outside ourselves. Neither our "soul-mates" nor bosses, peers, fans, bankers, families, friends nor pets hold this for us. Nor does ownership of chattel such as a Ferrari, Malibu ocean-side mansion, mega-yacht or Lear Jet. Nor do talents such as academic, athletic or musical prowess hold this for us. Only by going within, not without (external to ourselves), can we access highest-quality energy (including highest vitalization and truth – the truth of who we are at the core). Of course, the aforementioned tangible and intangible material props are nice – nothing wrong with any of them, especially if they support core truth (including life purpose and life service). But they cannot provide the quality of energy that may be accessed through profound self-awareness, meditation, breathing exercises, core creativity, etc. – which transform the core self. Know that we will not find the ultimate answers and energy by searching outside ourselves.

As "airy-fairy" as this may sound, experiences such as love of a soul-mate, respect of peers, procurement of desired objects, and mastery of academics and arts – can be satisfying experiences – yet the quality of these external sources of energy pales in comparison to the quality (potency, brilliance and benefit) of energy accessible through internal channels. Highest-quality energy is **indirectly** (only partially) accessed through external "energy" sources. In other words, you cannot reliably and completely access highest-quality energy through external means.

The great paradox reveals that direct access to highest-quality energy (light) is achieved through internal channels of access. Numerous ancient cultures believe that the practice of Stillness Meditation is an ultimate channel through which to **directly** access highest-quality energy. They believe that all other activities and experiences are **indirect** means of accessing energy. They believe that **all other experiences and activities are precursors to the practice and mastery of Stillness Meditation**. Stillness Meditation is always a unique experience. No two people practice or experience the process of meditation the same way. Nor are meditative journeys ever the same for any given individual, they are always different – yet the ultimate result is always the same . . . direct access to highest-quality energy (light) and its manifestations.

As a rule – the deeper within (a/k/a closer to the soul) the channel of access, the higher the quality of energy that may be accessed. The more superficial (egoic) the channel of access, the lower the quality of energy that may be accessed.

For example, the avenue of gossip is an extremely superficial/egoic channel of access to energy. Talking about other people, putting others down, to feel better about oneself is a practice engaged by people who feel insecure about themselves. Although insecure people may feel a momentary buzz by gossiping about others, the benefit is extremely temporary. Gossip provides nothing more than false energy. The ego feels a temporary surge of false power when gossiping about others.

An example of a moderately superficial channel of access to energy is romantic love (ignoring the component of unconditional love). As with gossip, the individual looks externally for an energy fix. However, unlike gossip, a moderate dosage of high-quality energy may be accessed when experiencing romantic love – if an aspect of the romantic love is unconditional (commensurate with a definition of love in which love is defined as an action through which one helps another to attain their highest spiritual development, in every instance, without exception).

An example of a minimally superficial channel of access to energy – though still through external means (with outer eyes open) – is exposure to sun or trees, which renders an indirect, yet beneficial, experience of light energy.

Internal access to light energy is the most direct path to highest-quality energy. Paradoxically, external access to light is an indirect source of light energy. Internal access is the direct source of (pure) light energy. So, a*ll externally-oriented activities are precursors to practice and mastery of (Stillness) Meditation* – an ultimate source of highest-quality energy (light).

* * *

A PRACTICAL TIP

To directly access highest-quality energy we must learn how to go within. To do so we must accomplish-as-best-we-can the Two Great Challenges of Personal Growth. First, we learn how to still the monkeymind. Second, we learn how to tap enhanced consciousness – via the soul. Use external sensory-stimulating supplements to facilitate this process. In sum, we align with the soul. Sound familiar? The recurring theme strikes again! There are prescribed steps to follow that support access to energy of progressively enhanced power and scope. These steps describe the protocol for alignment with the soul. And profound success.

PROGRESSION OF ACCESS TO ENERGY: Internal versus External Gateways. Internal gateways access energy of relatively greater power and concentration than external gateways of energy. In other words, we can receive greater vitalization and inspiration through internal focus, rather than by looking outside ourselves (for energy and inspiration).

It is incredibly challenging (a profound understatement) to open and master internal gateways of energy – which provide direct access to undiluted, pure energy (light). To do so, it typically is helpful to initially gain access to energy (of relatively diffuse quality) via external (indirect) gateways. This "primes the pump" of access to internal energy.

Energy influx
Begets
Energy influx

Induction of (true) energy into your bodymind's energetic pathways (regardless how diffuse) innately begets additional influx of energy. As an example, once we begin to learn an instrument – such as guitar – fingers gain dexterity and memory. Once the fingers gain mobility and memory, more difficult lessons can be tackled and conquered with progressively less effort. We become more efficient learners. Similarly, influx of energy into the bodymind's systems activates increasingly efficient attraction of energy (of enhanced quality). So, just like when learning guitar, wherein introductory lessons lead to intermediate and advanced lessons – and progressively enhanced benefit, it is the same for energy influx. The cumulative effect of exercise of introductory, external means for gaining energy eventually builds a solid foundation that serves to ease and strengthen practice of internal means of energetic influx. **External methods to access energy are the precursors of internal energetic gateways and, ultimately, Stillness Meditation.**

External (indirect) gateways to (true) energy provide wonderfully vitalizing energy, even though the energy holds relatively diminished concentration (with regard to energy accessed through internal means).

There is one <u>direct</u> (internal) source of purest, true energy,
There are two indirect (external) sources of pure, true energy,
And innumerable sources of false (illusory) energy.

LIGHT IS TRUE ENERGY. Recall that light particles are synonymous with energy particles. Everything is made of energy and, thereby, light (light particles and light waves). Light is either directly or indirectly accessed.

* * *

ANCILLARY CONCEPT

Light is information

In theory, since light particles are the building-blocks of everything, including theoretic time and space, light is believed to contain omniscient information (that spans all of theoretic time and space). Ancient cultures believed that Stillness Meditation innately accesses etheric rivers of infinite information (sometimes described as the Stream of Consciousness) that present themselves consciously and subconsciously through intuition, synchronicity, dreams . . . and miracles. Ancient philosophies believed that the truth of whom you are, including your core life purpose and life service, is accessed by quieting the monkeymind and tapping consciousness by initially using external sensory-stimulating supplements, the precursors to Stillness Meditation (that vertically align our inner geometry), and thereafter employing Stillness Meditation.

* * *

HIERARCHY OF ENERGY QUALITY. Pure light is highest quality energy – as light and energy are synonymous. Energy, may be accessed directly (through Stillness Meditation). Or indirectly – through interaction with nature, human beings, and objects. **Direct access to energy renders highest energetic purity. Indirect access to energy renders slightly diminished energetic purity (a bit more diffused energy) – which, like purest energy, is *extremely* beneficial.** Interaction with nature, human beings, and objects renders indirect access to true energy. Additionally these props serve as "triggers" (keys) to help us unbury, unlock, release and transcend necessary life lessons.

ENERGY SOURCES THAT FEED THE SOUL: Energy that feeds the soul is like a high-quality film. Memory of the film lasts a lifetime. And provides eternal benefit in the form of inspiration, helpful information, slight emotional triggering, and other positive attributes. Think of great movies you've seen. You can still recall certain scenes, characters, and the essence of the film, right? In essence, the movie lives on and on. Similarly, energy that serves the soul is timeless and infinitely beneficial.

Sources of energy that feed the soul include:

Unconditional love
Selfless, detached love for nature and people
(Support for the highest path of another)

Light
Inner light – via the inner eye

Sunlight
Outer light - via the physical eyes and body

Thought
Positive thought, intention, compassion, empathy
•
•   **Word**
Positive words of compassion, kindness, generosity

•   **Action**
Positive acts of compassion, kindness, generosity

•   **Creativity**
Art, music, dance (movement)

•   **Positivity**
Positive thought, word, action

Verticality (Soul-Alignment)
Vertically-aligned (soul-aligned) thought, word, action

- **Commitment aligned with life purpose**

- **Commitment aligned with life service**

- **Positive humor**

Effective communication
Honest, direct, loving

- **Triggers of buried emotion and energy**

ENERGY SOURCES THAT FEED THE EGO:

The ego (monkeymind) abhors uncertainty
To thwart uncertainty
The ego (monkeymind) takes any action necessary
To attain an illusory sense of control

Energy that feeds the ego is like a "bad" film. A scene or two from the film may seem entertaining, at best, in the moment – but the experience, the memory of the film, is forgotten by the time you leave the movie theatre. Except for any disturbing elements – which may linger in memory. In other words, you leave the theatre without memory of positive aspects of the film, and if you recall anything at all it will be only the negative aspects of the film – such as disturbing scenes, bad acting, cliché plot, or simply a sense of malaise for wasting $10 (plus the cost of popcorn) and two hours of this lifetime.

Energy that feeds the ego is fleeting (transitory), unaligned with truth, unaligned with core truth, and illusory. Examples of sources of energy that feed the ego include:

- **Self-focused thought, word, action**

- **Illusion**
Control is illusory

False sense of security

•   **Dominance over nature, people, objects**

•   **Attachment to materiality** (that does not support core purpose or service) Co-dependence upon people, objects, events, ideas

INTERNAL (DIRECT) SOURCES OF TRUE ENERGY. Stillness Meditation is a **direct** source of true energy (light), which is also described as consciousness, Universal energy, energy of Heaven and Earth, the Stream of Consciousness, etc. Stillness Meditation taps Universal consciousness – omniscient information that empowers the clarity and frequency of intuition, dreams, synchronicity . . . and miracles. The material benefits of Stillness Meditation, connection to the source of pure energy, are numerous and include physical health, emotional well-being (enhanced emotional release and awareness), increased vitality, and aligned success. Believe it or not.

* * *

ANCILLARY CONCEPT
Stillness Meditation:
Internal (Direct) Access to Heaven & Earth

What you focus upon
In the moment
Is all that you are.
Focus upon love
And you are love.
Focus upon hate
And you are hate.
Focus upon stillness
And your center is still.
Focus upon anger
And you are anger.

Stillness meditation is profound yet innate focus upon consciousness. One focuses not the external eyes and technical, material-oriented thinking but, rather, focuses the "inner eye" and soul-aligned bodymind. Meditation focuses upon the energies of Heaven and Earth. The energies of Heaven and Earth are vertically-aligned (aligned with soul) – extending infinitely high, to the distant reaches of the universe, and as low as the center of the Earth. **Innate focus upon Heaven and Earth, through meditation, automatically aligns the energies of the soul and bodymind in a vertical array, connecting our energies with Heaven and Earth. In theory, this brings infinite light and wisdom to us from Heaven, and grounding energy from Earth.**

Focus is binary. So, by definition, when focused in Stillness Meditation we are not focused upon the ego (egoic aspect of personality). We may focus on either soul-essence (thought, word, action) or ego-essence (thought, word, action) – but not both.

Stillness Meditation is soul-focus. Although the soul is always connected to consciousness, we are not always able to sense consciousness – as we often focus (whether aware of it or not) on ego – which blocks connection to the soul. Stillness Meditation is soul-focus – which trumps egoic resistance and blockage to the wisdom and guidance of the soul.

Profound meditation opens an energetic bridge that extends from Heaven to Earth, and vice-versa, via the soul and longitudinal center of the bodymind.

The mechanics of the energetic flow of profound Stillness Meditation follow. First, the energy of Heaven vertically descends to a center of electromagnetic activity, located approximately twelve inches above the crown of the head. Ancient philosophers described this location as the Soul Star. They believed that the consciousness of the soul approximates this area. Next, after the energy of Heaven connects with the center of the Soul Star (Eighth Chakra), the energy then descends through the center of the bodymind, descending down an energetic column situated just anterior to the spinal column – beginning atop the crown of the head (Crown Chakra), then through the center of the head (Third-Eye Chakra), throat (Throat Chakra), heart (Heart Chakra), solar plexus (Third Chakra), navel center (Second Chakra) and perineum (Root Chakra). Then down from the perineum (groin) to the center of the Earth. In this way, Stillness Meditation hooks us up to a subtle yet profound electromagnetic circuit that extends from Heaven to Earth and back to Heaven – though the precise center of the bodymind. Connecting us to Heaven's wisdom, guidance of soul-connected consciousness, and the grounding wisdom and energy of Earth.

The term "chakra" is translated in Sanskrit as "spinning vortex." Or spinning wheel. Chakras are electromagnetic centers centered in the body, which radiate outward. Chakras 1 through 6 radiate forward and back, and Chakra 7 radiates upward – in the shape of funnels (vortices). There are seven major chakras in the body. The chakras spin at different rates, with the lower chakras spinning more slowly. Chakras describe different attributes of the human psyche' and persona.

Stillness Meditation helps to "dissolve" the ego. We bypass ego-focus when engaged in profound meditation. Unfortunately, profound meditation can be a challenging condition to attain. It is difficult for many of us to sit still, much less quiet the mind – and connect to higher consciousness. But, **there are precursors to meditation that help open us to progressively deeper inner stillness. These are external sensory-stimulating supplements** – tools that align us with the vertical nature of the soul and consciousness. They help us connect to stillness, via the soul (and connection to the present moment). And help us ultimately draw Heaven's infinite wisdom and electromagnetic energy down to us, and the Earth's grounding wisdom and electromagnetic energy up to us (via energy meridians that flow up through the ball of the foot, and flow down through the heel of the foot – pursuant to Qi Gong theory).

* * *

TWO INDIRECT (EXTERNAL) SOURCES OF TRUE ENERGY: Beautiful, vitalizing, healthful energy may be accessed by reaching outside ourselves *(in an appropriate manner)*. The four external sources of true energy are Heaven, Earth, nature, and human beings (only that aspect of dynamic is based in unconditional love). Since Heaven and Earth may be directly accessed (via internal energy gates), we shall consider only the latter two sources of energy, namely nature and the unconditional aspect of human love, as external sources of energy.

External access to energy is indirect. In other words, **when we reach outside ourselves for energy, the energy we access is less pure – of lower concentration – than when we "go within" for energy.** External sources of energy are less efficient (less direct and pure) than internal sources of energy. Internal sources of energy are a direct path to consciousness (light energy via connection to Heaven and Earth). External sources require an additional, intermediate step to access light energy. External sources access the positive energy of nature and/or people, and may harness unconditional loving consciousness (the energy of Heaven and Earth that may be accessed through human interaction) via these props (nature and people). Internal access to energy more directly taps into consciousness, the energy of Heaven and Earth. Light.

Initially, it is easiest to tap positive energy through external props. Influx of positive energy through external sources helps inspire subsequent internal access to positive energetic inflow.

ILLUSION IS FALSE ENERGY. The soul sees things as they truly are. The ego does not. The ego filters truth through the clouded veil of its density/skewed biases/woundedness, and thereby interprets all of creation in an illusory, untruthful way. The soul is crystal clear, unbiased, healthy. Soul sees eternal, infinite truth in every moment. The interpretations and beliefs of ego (the egoic aspect of the personality) are neither reliable, insightful, nor helpful. Interpretations of the soul are always reliable, insightful and honest. The ego's illusory interpretations render false information and false energy. The soul's truthful interpretations render true energy.

Chapter Three

SOUL-ALIGNMENT

THE FOUNDATION OF HUMAN EXISTENCE, AND SO THE PHYSICAL STRUCTURE OF THE HUMAN BEING, IS VERTICAL ALIGNMENT. The spine and nervous system are tangible mirror reflections of the intangible (etheric) inner energetic pattern of verticality.

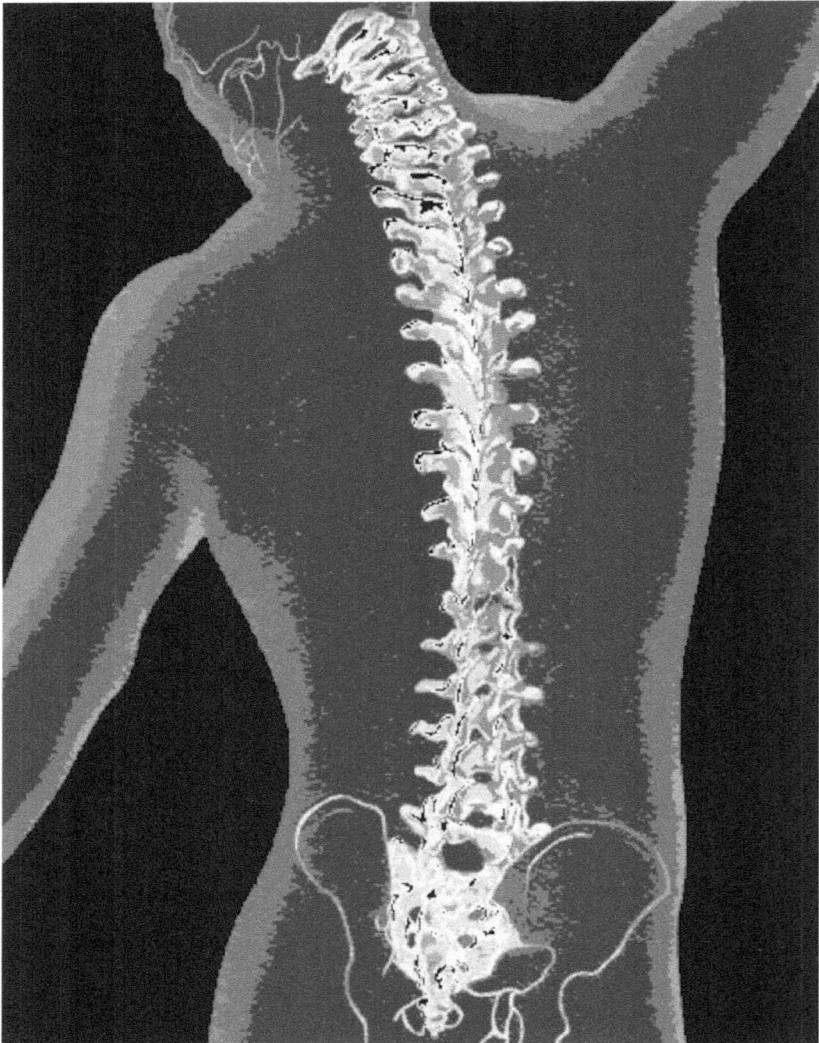

Energy of the (healthy) spine is vertically-aligned.

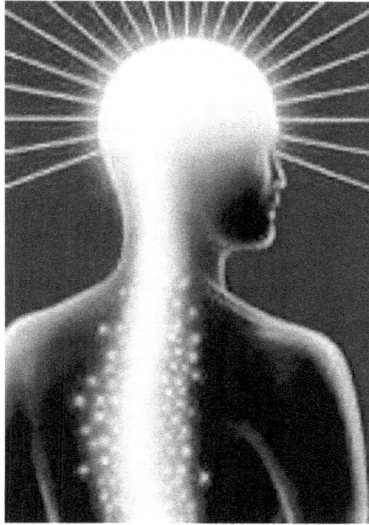

Energy of the (healthy) bodymind is vertically-aligned.

Just as Cerebrospinal Fluid flows up and down the (healthy) spinal column, energetic waveforms move up and down the (healthy) bodymind. Similar to Cerebrospinal Fluid, which courses unrestricted through the spine, delivering healthy nutrients and minerals – energy courses through the bodymind, delivering healthy energy (light, unconditional love, conscious information, health) to all levels of the human organism including the aura.

> *"Blood follows energy."*
> — Traditional Chinese Medicine

PHYSICAL FLOW FOLLOWS FLOW OF INTENTION. Intention is powerful. What we intend – ultimately happens (as long as our intention is aligned with the will of natural order) . . . so we must be careful what we wish for! If we wish to heal, we shall (again, if aligned with the will of natural order – i.e., if this outcome inspires, or is inspired by, a helpful lesson that the soul has not yet resolved/mastered). If we wish not to heal, surely we shall not. The point is – intention causes things to happen. Recall that two-thirds of intention is subconscious (karmic) and one-third is conscious – so, we must clean up our inner landscape, to preclude further cause (innate attraction) of un-preferred consequences (harsh lessons). We must learn to use intention wisely. Intend soul-aligned (vertical) energetic flow. This causes (attracts) health, success, happiness and joy. And, most notably, bliss – unabashed connection to Heaven and Earth via the bodymind (chakras). *With each breath, intend vertical flow – and immediately and completely we become soul-aligned (for that moment). Connected to the core self. Paradoxically, we connect so deeply to the core of who we are that you tap the Infinite (Heaven and Earth).*

Intend vertical flow to *be* vertical flow. Recall that all we focus upon in the moment is all that we are. Vertical flow (soul-alignment) begets health on every level – as vertical flow is health. Vitality. Life itself.

As an example, blood flow is preceded by energetic flow. Blood follows energy. Energetic flow is guided by intention – of both conscious and subconscious dimension. Intention to align the core self vertically (aligned with the directionality of the spine, nervous system, and core energy systems) innately aligns us with the intention to heal. This inspires healing energy to flow freely that, in turn, inspires blood to flow. Blood carries minerals and elements necessary for healing. Healing occurs. So, intention to align with vertical flow automatically inspires physical healing and profound, soul-aligned success.

* * *

ANCILLARY CONCEPT:

Vertical Alignment –
The Spine, Central Channel and Antahkarana

Contemporary Chiropractors and numerous ancient philosophies believe(d) that vertical energetic flow is essential to physical, emotional and spiritual health. Chiropractors consider the spinal column to be the energetic core of the self. Taoists believe that the Central Channel, a vertical energy meridian flowing from the crown of the head through the perineum (groin) – located just anterior to the spine at the body's mid-line, is our energetic core. The ancient Tibetans described essentially the same energy meridian as the Antahkarana, a path that connects Heaven to Earth, via the center of each of the seven major chakras in the bodymind. Unimpeded energetic flow through the vertical spine, Central Column, and Antahkarana promotes physical, emotional, and spiritual health according to Chiropractors, Taoists, and ancient Tibetans, respectively.

Traditional Chinese Medical theory and practice (Taoist practices of acupuncture, herbal science, and Qi Gong, the science of energy flow) parallel theory and therapeutic application of the ancient, esoteric Tibetan notion of the Antahkarana – a bridge that connects Heaven to the center of the Earth, via the precise center of each of the seven major chakras, located in the physical body.

Ancient esoteric Tibetan healers (energy therapists) purportedly could diagnose physical, emotional and spiritual maladies based upon their perceived sense of the shape of the energetic Antahkarana. Where the form of the Antahkarana wasn't in perfect vertical alignment – where there was a curve, kink, and/or skew in the vertical symmetry of the Antahkarana – they could diagnose specific physical, emotional or spiritual imbalances, dysfunctions and/or disease, whether or not the condition had yet outwardly (physically) manifested (as dysfunction and disease follow energetic stagnancy and imbalance). Diagnosis based upon verticality of energy and inconsistencies in vertical patterns allowed the practitioner to foresee illness before it surfaced – enhancing the probability of success of preventive care.

* * *

Recall that waveforms assume various shapes. They frequently travel in spiral or linear form. The core of the human body, the spinal column, is designed to parallel the alignment of vertical core waveforms. Vertical waveforms represent health.

*The seven major (chakra) energetic centers of the body
are spinning vortices – vertically aligned.*

CLOSER LOOK AT ALIGNMENT OF THE (HEALTHY) BODYMIND REVEALS NOT SIMPLY VERTICAL LINES OF ENERGY BUT, IN ADDITION, VERTICAL ALIGNMENT OF ENERGETIC VORTICES. Recall that vortices are spiraling waveforms that are frequently observed in all levels of nature – especially with regard to primordial, rudimentary aspects of nature. Both the "macro" – the universe, and the "micro" – the human body, developed from vortices. Recall that galaxies, galactic black holes, and DNA are comprised of energetic vortices. In theory, these vortices are vertically-aligned with the soul.

* * *

**ANCILLARY CONCEPT
More on the Antahkarana**

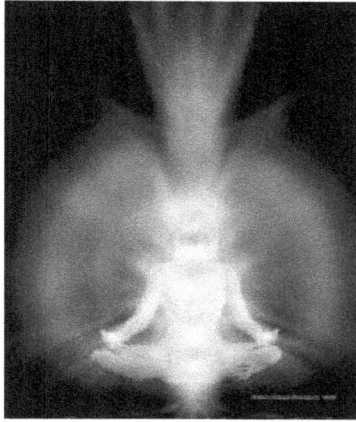

Energy of the healthy Antahkarana,
Bridge to Heaven and Earth
Via the BodyMind
Is comprised of vertically-aligned
Lines of Force
And
Spheres of Influence.
Like a May-Pole.

The Antahkarana is the bodymind's vertical energetic connection to Heaven and Earth (poetic Taoist descriptions of universal and grounding energies, respectively).

FUNCTION. The Antahkarana IS our inner landscape – and its connection to the outer world (and entire universe). Specifically, **the Antahkarana is both the energetic blueprint of our inner landscape and its connection to the outer world. The center-line-of-the-Antahakarana is vertical – in theory extending from Heaven to Earth through the precise center of the bodymind. This energetic center-line is the blueprint of our inner energetic landscape. The inner energetic template is a mirror reflection of the state of our conscious mentality, conscious emotionality, and subconscious aspects.**

The greater the degree of mental and emotional evolution, the straighter the center-line of the Antahkarana. This is the objective barometer of personal evolution.

To Eastern philosophers, the (objective) goal of life is to maintain perfect vertical alignment of the center-line of the Antahkarana. This is the objective standard that defines Enlightenment (Ascension).

*So, perfect inner **verticality** is the standard that defines highest evolution – the foundation of profound (soul-aligned) success.*

Perfect vertical alignment of the center-line-of-the-Antahkarana is synonymous with "Ascension" – raising ("ascending") inner energetic vibration to the highest degree possible. More detail regarding "vibration" (vibrational medicine and vibrational science) is described later.

ENLIGHTENMENT IS AN OBJECTIVE SCIENCE – NOT A SUBJECTIVE DESCRIPTION. The degree of verticality of the center-line-of-the-Antahkarana **objectively** defines our degree of evolution.

WHY DO EVOLUTION AND ENLIGHTENMENT (A/K/A ASCENSION) MATTER?
Recall that our inner landscape creates our outer world experience. How is this possible? **How can our inner energy posture and movements affect the outer world? The simplicity of the physical structure of the Antahkarana succinctly reveals this great secret.**

"Form follows function."

— Anonymous

PHYSICAL STRUCTURE OF THE ANTAHKARANA. The form of the Antahkarana reflects the straightforward mechanics of this energetic bridge. The Antahkarana looks like a "maypole." A maypole is a large schoolyard gadget that consists of a tall center-pole that extends as high as a schoolyard swing-set, with many ropes affixed to the top of the pole. Children hold the ends of the ropes as they run in circles around the pole (hopefully in the same direction!) The Antahkarana looks like a maypole except that the spiraling ropes (i.e., vortices) are affixed to any point on the center-pole, not simply to the top of the center-pole (as in the case of the maypole).

The Antahkarana consists of "Lines of Force" (a vertically-oriented center-line – like the center-pole of the maypole) and "Spheres of Influence" (spiraling vortices – like the ropes attached to the maypole).

Lines of Force
Our inner energetic blueprint.
A precise map of our inner landscape.
The vertical bridge
Connecting Heaven to Earth
Via the bodymind.

LINES OF FORCE – OUR INNER ENERGETIC TEMPLATE. Energy from Heaven descends to the bodymind (as inspired by *intention, inhalation and other vertically-aligned techniques and external sensory-stimulating supplements)*, by initially entering the precise center of the crown of the head (Crown Chakra). The universal energy then descends through the precise center of each of the other (six) major chakras, before exiting via the lower aspect of the bodymind (heels of the feet) and descending into the (center of the) core of the Earth. In other words, Heavenly energy descends via the bodymind to ground in the Earth.

Meanwhile, simultaneous to the descension of Heavenly energy to the core of the Earth via the bodymind, Earth energy ascends through the balls of the feet, piercing the precise center of the perineum/groin (Root Chakra), and then ascends through the precise center of the other six major chakras, before exiting the Crown Chakra to return to Heaven. In other words, Earthly energy rises through the bodymind to meet Heaven.

In sum, Lines of Force, vertically-aligned energetic meridians, connect Heavenly energy to Earth, and Earthly energy to Heaven – via the bodymind. So, Lines of Force accomplish two great tasks. First, they serve to energize and ground the bodymind – causing the bodymind to become a "conduit" of the wisdom and energy of Heaven and Earth. Second, they connect Heaven to Earth, and vice-versa.

The degree of verticality of Lines of Force defines our state of evolution. Perfect vertical alignment reflects a state of Enlightenment. Less-than-perfect alignment mirrors (and maps) unresolved inner energetic conflict, dysfunction and disease. More on this later.

Spheres of Influence
Our connection to the outer world.
Spiraling bridges
That span from our inner energetic landscape
To all aspects of the universe.

SPHERES OF INFLUENCE – OUR CONNECTION TO THE OUTER WORLD. Whereas Lines of Force serve as the vertical center-line of the maypole-like Antahkarana, Spheres of Influence are vortices that extend, in spiral fashion, from all points on Lines of Force to all reaches of the universe. Spheres of Influence are our connection to the outer world. Spheres of Influence bridge the gap from our inner landscape to the outer world.

INTERACTION OF LINES OF FORCE AND SPHERES OF INFLUENCE. Lines of Force are our inner blueprint. Spheres of Influence are bridges that connect our inner blueprint to the outer world. Lines of Force provide universal and grounding energies that empower and inspire the scope and character of the spiraling Spheres of Influence as they reach, like spiraling tentacles, to every corner of the universe. **Lines of Force mirror, and concurrently define, who we are (*in each moment*). As we shift and transform in every moment, so do Lines of Force.** *The greater the degree of inner evolution, the more vertical the alignment of Lines of Force.* **Spheres of Influence are spirals of communication "wire" that TRANSMIT to the outer world (telling the world who we are) AND RECEIVE worldly information. Lines of Force DEFINE who we are.** Spheres of Influence communicate "who we are" to the world.

THE PRECISE SHAPE OF LINES OF FORCE EXPLAIN THE POLARITIES OF EVERYDAY HUMAN EXPERIENCE – THE UPS, THE DOWNS, AND THE POLAR EXTREMES WITNESSED IN DAILY LIVING.

The shape of the center-line (Lines of Force) of the Antahkarana explains the degree of polarity (extreme situations) that we experience in the world. For example, non-vertical kinks in the "relationship" area of the Antahkarana attract guys/girls to date whose attributes may vary greatly (from one person to the next) – helping us to learn more about ourselves (by mirroring the unhealed qualities of our polarized egoic aspects of personality). As we heal these issues, the kinks in the Antahkarana are straightened (energetically resolved).

Experience is a great teacher
As it facilitates eventual mastery
Of essential life lessons.

Extreme situations are designed to cause (extreme) learning – by necessity. Of course, trial-and-error learning is not the preferred way to learn. But, nonetheless, at times – especially when we're really stuck in an unhealthy pattern that, it seems, may never end – a difficult trial may be the only way to finally *see things as they truly are*, crushing illusions, ultimately causing awakening to truth (which prior we were not yet ready to see and/or accept) – which serves to break the unhealthy pattern. Trial-and-error learning may not be much fun – but it can be effective – especially when lessons to be learned are extreme.

Natural order abhors a vacuum.
Natural order shall always provide
Whatever resources you need
To further learning and personal evolution
Except (linear) time.
Linear time is the only scarce,
irreplaceable resource.

Natural order shall always replace
All that you falsely believed were lost
Unless the person, object or event
No longer serves your evolution.

The only cost of trial-and-error learning, in the long-run, is… (worldly, linear) time. We are eternally presented with repetitive lessons until we gain mastery of these essential lessons. So, we are presented resources necessary to help us learn these lessons. The only resource that we are not given is additional material time. Trial-and-error learning takes (linear) time.

The ups, downs and extremes experienced in daily living are the result of the magnetic power of the center-line (the Lines of Force) of the Antahkarana. *Wherever a kink defers the verticality of Lines of Force, we subsequently attract/create an experience designed to help us remove the kink from the Lines of Force – by causing us to resolve (heal) the underlying issue that caused the non-vertical kink in the Lines of Force.* In other words, the experience we attract helps us straighten the Lines of Force to a more vertical posture (by straightening – "verticalizing" - the unresolved issue that caused the kink).

The extreme polarities experienced in daily life all-too-frequently accompany the process of resolution of challenging life lessons. When we face a challenging life lesson, like choosing a lifemate or career path, our reactions and subsequent choices may vacillate wildly from one extreme to the other. This emotional and mental reactivity is energetically reflected as a (non-vertical) kink in Lines of Force – the blueprint within.

As a specific example, imagine you are dating a person who you realize (after around ninety days of courtship) seems to be afraid of commitment. [Note that The Ninety-Day Rule states that it takes approximately ninety days to see the "other side" (shadow aspect of the egoic personality) of anyone with whom we relate to (closely) – whether at work, or in friendship, family, or romance. After ninety days of interpersonal dynamic, you may observe that people express subtle-yet-specific patterns of emotional reactivity. See *Conscious Relationship* by this author.] This may be due to fear of engulfment – fear of intimacy; i.e., when you get close (s)he seems to run away. Then suppose you date someone who wants you to be close, but possibly a bit too close or a bit too often. In other words, their emotional reaction to relationship seems to be the extreme opposite from the preceding person. The immediate reason beneath this is rather simple: your Lines of Force had a kink which reflects *your* egoic personality's unresolved dynamics in relationship – and this kink attracted gals/guys ("triggers") who will help you to resolve the kink in your Lines of Force, the reflection of your unresolved relational issues. In other words, the (wo)men serve as mirrors of your own unresolved inner fears of engulfment and abandonment – polar aspects of the same core issue.

We experience people who express
Extreme reactions
As they mirror the inner blueprint
Of our own unresolved extreme reactivity.

Our egos experience polarized reactivity
Regarding any issues
That our egos have not yet resolved.

We attract others who express great reactivity
To remind us of our own reactivity
So we can heal, resolve, and evolve
And thereby innately straighten the Antahkarana

The core reason why we experience extreme situations is that they help us to heal the unresolved, (extremely) reactive/volatile aspects of our egoic personalities. **The ego acts in the extreme – and the ego's reactivity swings so wildly that its retorts cover the extreme ends of the spectrum.** For example, the ego experiences both fear of abandonment AND fear of engulfment. It's merely a matter of degree as to which reaction it expresses (and experiences) more frequently and consciously. So, although a person may express fear of abandonment more frequently – as this may be the more conscious reaction – they also experience fear of engulfment – although this fear may reside in a more-or-less dormant state in the subconscious (shadow) aspect of the egoic personality. Whenever one's emotional reactions are out-of-balance, both ends of the spectrum of reactivity exist, one is conscious and thereby obvious, the other is subconscious and thereby relatively dormant (less obvious).

THE IMPORTANT POINT TO REMEMBER IS THAT KINKS IN THE ANTAHKARANA'S CENTER-LINE, THE LINES OF FORCE, INDICATE UNRESOLVED ASPECTS OF THE EGOIC PERSONALITY.

For this reason, gifted healers are able to "read" the Antahkarana, diagnose where unresolved issues lay, and pro-actively heal the issues – so as to preclude the need for subsequent challenging trial-and-error experiences. *By pro-actively healing the issue, there is no need to attract outer world "triggers" (people, objects and events that cause you to react) to facilitate healing in the material world via trial-and-error experience (as the issue is already internally – "energetically" - resolved). This saves you time, distraction and suffering – while enhancing personal evolution and material standing.*

SO, WHY DOES THIS SEEMINGLY ESOTERIC STUFF MATTER? WHY IS IT IMPORTANT TO UNDERSTAND THE NUANCES OF THE ANTAHKARANA, LINES OF FORCE, AND SPHERES OF INFLUENCE? HOW DOES THIS IMPACT OUR EVERYDAY LIVES? HOW CAN WE BETTER OUR LIVES BY APPLYING THIS ANCIENT TECHNOLOGY?

We cannot control the outer world.
We cannot control people, objects or events.
But, the good news is that
We can control our inner landscape.
We influence the shape of our inner Lines of Force
Which influence the ups, downs, and extremes
Witnessed in daily living.
Believe this.

The concept of "control" in the material world is nothing more than a wishful illusion. We can control nothing in this world except our inner template. Fortunately, our inner work exerts powerful influence over our outer experience. Don't simply take my word for it – test this theory ... practice exercises that enhance the vertical alignment of your inner template – the Lines of Force – and you will gain firsthand material evidence of the power of this ancient technology in your everyday life.

IN SUMMARY, THERE ARE TWO WAYS TO GAIN MASTERY OF FUNDAMENTAL AND ADVANCED LIFE LESSONS.

1)   Trial-and-error repetition of challenging situations – that are attracted (created) by the magnetic force of the kinked deviations in the center-line of the Antahkarana (Lines of Force);

OR

2)   Pro-active mastery of the inner self – synonymous with pro-active straightening of Lines of Force via alleviation of kinks in the Lines of Force. Pro-active (inner) self-mastery precludes the need to magnetically attract extreme life situations that serve to challenge and ultimately teach us via difficult life trials.

The choice is ours – in each moment.

* * *

ENERGY PATTERNS MAY BE INFLUENCED. Although a singular particle of energy may be neither created nor destroyed, energetic patterns *may* be influenced. Utilization of external sensory-stimulating supplements affects energetic wave patterns that, in turn, influence the inner (subconscious and conscious) landscape and magnetic attraction of subsequent external conditions. Intention, words, and actions influence energy patterns. Vertical intention, words, and actions create vertical energy patterns – the foundation of health, vitality, and success.

ENERGETIC WAVEFORM PATTERNS MAY BE INFLUENCED IN THREE WAYS. We can create (congeal particles to form a waveform), destroy (dissipate waveforms back to particle form), or simply modify waveforms. As an example, we can cause energetic waveforms to appear – seemingly from nowhere. In extreme instances, spontaneous creation of waveforms may be described as nothing short of miraculous (miracles!) And, we can cause energetic waveforms to disappear (release of stagnant energies such as stuck emotions).

WHY IS IT VALUABLE TO KNOW HOW TO INFLUENCE ENERGY PATTERNS? Because energy is the building-block of everything. So, if we can influence energy, we can influence

everything. For instance, we can create miracles (a/k/a creation of energetic waveforms where prior there were none). We can release illness (disappearance of waves of stagnant energy).

Careful what you wish for . . .

A BRIEF DIGRESSION REGARDING MANIFESTATION: Know that we have the inherent power to manifest *anything* we desire – as long as it serves our highest interest (from the perspective of natural order). Yet – please heed a word of caution regarding the definition of "highest interest." Our highest interest is *whatever experience best serves the soul (a/k/a our truth) in the long-run in the physical, mental, emotional and spiritual planes.* So, any experiences that serve to further learning and growth at the levels of the personality (helping the egoic personality to release and align with soul) and the soul (helping us to connect more easily and completely with soul, Heaven and Earth), are considered to be in the soul's highest interest.

The goal of life is to learn, connect, and grow at the soul level. The soul is the true self. The conscious self. So, if we desire something that does not serve our soul's highest interest, odds do not favor attainment or receipt of the desired outcome. If we desire something that serves our highest interest – and perform the appropriate thoughts, words and actions (with mindfulness and focus upon body-centered breath) in each moment – it may be achieved. But we must choose carefully – for we just may receive what we ask for. If we ask from the perspective of the egoic personality, the result may not serve us in the long-run, rendering an uncomfortable eventual result. If we ask from the depths of the soul, the soul will be given what it needs – given we take right action to accomplish the requisite steps.

THE GEOMETRIC ALIGNMENT OF THE ENERGY OF THE SOUL IS

V
E
R
T
I
C
A
L

THE GEOMETRIC ALIGNMENT OF THE PRESENT MOMENT IS

V
E
R
T
I
C
A
L

Numerous ancient cultures describe the soul as a brilliant star-like energy center. The "Soul Star," as it is known, is located approximately twelve inches above the crown of the head. The soul star is bisected by the Antahkarana, the vertical ray that connects Heaven to Earth via the bodymind's seven major chakras. The soul star is known as the Eighth Chakra, and is the first major chakra located outside (above) the physical aspect of the bodymind. Recall that the etheric aspect of the bodymind extends infinitely to all corners of the universe via Spheres of Influence – hence, the soul is located well-within the boundaries of the etheric aspect of the bodymind.

*The point is that the soul is located directly above the head – in a position that resides **along a vertical line** (the Antahkarana) that pierces the crown (and all other chakras). Since the soul is positioned in a vertical line above the bodymind, the **soul is accessed only by vertical intention (thought), word and action. In other words, our truth (the true core self) may be accessed through vertically-aligned activity.***

THE SOUL IS ACCESSED VIA VERTICAL WAVEFORMS. Only vertically-oriented activities – in the form of *vertical thoughts, words and/or actions* – access the soul. By definition, vertically-aligned activities are thoughts, words and actions that create soul-aligned (vertical) waveforms. These waveforms transcend (ascend from) the bodymind in a vertical vector, traveling up the Lines of Force of the Antahkarana, and pierce the (relatively) vertically-positioned soul.

Vertically-oriented activities are performed in the material plane by the soul-aligned aspect of the personality. In contrast, the egoic personality performs horizontally-aligned activities (which resist and counter the wisdom and guidance of the soul). Thoughts, words and actions that counter the wisdom of the soul add to mental and emotional clutter.

VERTICALLY-ORIENTED ACTIVITIES CONSTITUTE "RIGHT ACTION" (as defined by Tibetan Lama Arjia Rinpoche). When I studied and meditated in the Mill Valley (California) home of the wise, kind and generous lama, I observed that he silently asks himself "what is right action?" – In every waking moment. An incredible discipline. Right action is that activity that best serves the interests of all humanity and the universe, in the greatest possible way, in every given moment. Hence, right action may vary from moment to moment.

Examples of vertically-aligned activities are described in the chapter entitled "External sensory-stimulating supplements."

The Infinite
Is the Mother of the Present Moment.
The Present Moment is the Mother of the Soul.
Soul is the Mother of Vertical Activity.

To Access Presence
And Innately Connect to the Infinite
(Natural Order, Highest Inspiration)
Ascend the Lineage
In Reverse

Exercise Vertical Activity
To Access Soul
Which Ignites Presence
And Connects Us
To the Infinite

SOUL-ALIGNED (VERTICAL) ACTIVITY IS THE FOUNDATION OF PRESENT MOMENT FOCUS (A/K/A MINDFULNESS). Vertical activity makes it easier to focus upon the present moment – by causing the body and mind's energies to align vertically. We feel more relaxed and connected to ourselves (body, higher mind, and soul) when practicing vertical activity. This is an indicator of present moment focus. For example, after taking a long run, working for hours on an artistic project, creating music, or dancing (or challenging athletic endeavors) – do you notice that you feel more "in" your body (i.e., grounded), and mentally at peace – i.e., do you observe that your mind is no longer cluttered with scattered, distracting thoughts? **This is the power of vertical (soul-aligned) activity.** *V**ertical activity – thought, words and action – takes us into the now.* The now (present-moment mindfulness) is home to the soul, core truth, our unique life purpose and life service, intimacy, true love, vital health, prosperity and all other measures of profound (true) success. Each moment that we are engaged in vertically-aligned thought, word and action, we innately activate presence and soul consciousness – as vertical alignment causes our inner energy template to automatically ascend (in the moment) to the level of the Eighth Chakra, the Soul Star – the soul (located twelve inches above the crown of the head) . . . and beyond.

Recall the Taoist saying: *"All that you focus upon (and intend, say and do) in this moment is all that you are."* Ancient Taoists believed that all that exists is this moment. They believed that tomorrow is not real as it never arrives (it is merely a figment of the biases of the imagination), and that the past is not real – as the memory of yesterday is nothing more than your biased interpretation of what you think occurred – which is not absolute truth and, therefore, is not reliable. In sum, so-called past and so-called future are not real, as they are merely illusions of the mind (future is imaginary and past is not accurately remembered). For these reasons, **the Taoists recognize only the present moment, the now, as real.**

THE LINEAGE OF EVOLUTION

The Infinite
Is the Mother of the Present Moment.
The Present Moment is the Mother of the Soul.
Soul is the Mother of Vertical Activity.

TO EVOLVE (A/K/A ASCEND), WE SIMPLY REVERSE THE ORDER OF THE LINEAGE OF EVOLUTION – AND WORK OUR WAY UP THE EVOLUTIONARY SEQUENCE. In other words, the practice of vertical activity aligns us with the wisdom of the soul. Soul-alignment causes us to automatically focus upon the present moment. Presence (present moment mindfulness) causes us to connect to highest inspiration, the Infinite. In sum, vertical activity begets connection to soul, presence and inspiration.

For example, recall the inner discipline of Tibetan Lama Arjia Rinpoche who practices constant meditation upon "right action." He asks himself "what is right action?" in every moment (meanwhile he focuses upon his breath which helps him to maintain his eternal meditation – more on Breathwork later). And believes that what you focus on in any moment, is all that you are. If you focus on anger, you ARE anger. If you focus on peace, you ARE peace. So, in other words, he asks himself what the most helpful (from a global perspective) thought, word or action might be in every moment. And, then actually DOES just that. He has disciplined his mind to then pursue a specific thought (positive), utter specific words, or perform specific actions – that are most helpful to humanity, regardless how subtle the degree of benefit, and which in turn cause his inner energy to ascend (evolve) vertically. Which then begets even greater connection to core truth, prescription of further vertical activity based upon greater depth of insight, etc? An endless, positive, synergistic loop. Of course, it takes time to develop this level of internal discipline and energetic integrity.

The wisdom of the soul subtly guides us to exercise vertical activity, which innately helps us to focus more consistently in the present moment. *It is extremely difficult to be present (mindful) without the proactive practice of vertical (soul-aligned) activity.* For example, I sometimes find it easier to sit in Stillness Meditation after I have worked out, hiked outdoors, practiced yoga, created music, and/or danced prior to sitting. The preceding exercise (kinesthetic, musical, artistic, or natural – in an outdoor setting) helps me to still (bypass) my monkeymind beforehand, making it much easier to sit and meditate. From an objective, scientific perspective, the vertical activity causes the energy in the bodymind to ascend vertically, beforehand, easing the transition from profane consciousness to meditative consciousness.

SOUL-ALIGNED (VERTICAL) THOUGHT, WORD AND ACTION ALWAYS FOCUSES UPON THE PRESENT MOMENT. Vertically-aligned activities do not focus upon so-called past or future. For example, have you ever observed during a tough work-out that your thoughts regarding past and future dissipate and that by the end of the workout your mind seems clearer? This is presence (and grounding – contact with Earth energy via body-based activity).

Presence *feels* good. More aptly, presence feels GREAT! The mind is clear of cluttered thought (thought regarding so-called past and future). Worry regarding (so-called) future uncertainty and confusion, regret or over-analysis regarding the (so-called) past dissolve. The clouds dissipate. *We feel rather than think.* The feeling of our connection to the body, Earth and self awakens. Details that once seemed so important suddenly don't seem to matter nearly as much. The breath deepens. The tone of the voice may lower a bit. The rhythm of thought slows. A sense of serenity naturally envelopes us. We are present. Thanks to vertical thought, word and action.

To the Yogi and meditator, presence is transcendent. In everyday living and routine, presence innately brings comfort, grounding, clarity of mind, ease of decision-making, inner peace, harmony . . . and comprehensive success.

Present moment-focus is synonymous with soul-focus. To be present, focused upon the present moment, we must access the soul. To access the soul, we must be present. *The soul is always focused (a/k/a resides) in the present moment.*

IN CONTRAST, THE UNALIGNED, EGOIC PERSONALITY IS ALWAYS FOCUSED UPON EITHER (SO-CALLED) PAST OR FUTURE. The ego falsely believes that co-called past and future are real. So it remains steadily focused upon fear and worry regarding future uncertainty. And remains focused upon mis-interpretation, over-analysis and regret of past experiences.

HOW CAN WE SHORT-CIRCUIT THE POWER OF THE EGO? In theory, the ego is easily defeated (bypassed). Recall that soul and ego (egoic personality) are mutually exclusive. They are binary. In each moment, we are focused upon either soul or ego. One or the other. So, **it is merely a question of focus. If we focus on ego and its allies** (so-called past, so-called future, resistance to guidance by the soul, unaligned activity in the forms of unaligned thought, word and action), **we empower ego.** We are ego. **If we focus on soul and its allies (the present moment and aligned, vertical activity), we empower the soul.** We are soul.

Simply, **ego is defeated (bypassed) by vertical activity.** More precisely, ego's efforts to block truth and success are short-circuited by vertical activity. Ego is always focused upon either so-called past or future. **Vertical thought, word and action bypass ego by automatically bringing our attention to the present moment.** Soul or ego. We make this choice each moment. It is up to us whether we connect to soul, or are limited by ego. In each moment we make this choice whether aware of this fact or not. We choose either on a proactive, conscious, affirmative basis – or by default (by not making a choice, we still choose – in which case we connect to limitation caused by resistance that accompanies ego-focus).

The energetic clouds
Of confused thought, emotion and limitation
are horizontal.
Like an overcast sky.

THE EGO (EGOIC ASPECT OF THE PERSONALITY, MONKEYMIND) IS THE SUM OF ALL HORIZONTAL WAVEFORMS. From a scientific perspective, the energy of unaligned thoughts, words and actions – activities that are out-of-sync (unaligned) with the guidance of the soul, create (and are created by) horizontal energies. Horizontal energies impinge, rather than support, ascension of inner energy. Horizontal (a/k/a unaligned) energies cause the Lines of Force of the Antahkarana to kink, to waver from a straight vertical form. This causes resistance and blockage to (vertically-oriented) guidance by the soul.

Mundane, limited and confused thoughts and emotion cause horizontally-oriented shifts in our inner energetic template. The unaligned aspect of the personality, the egoic personality, is horizontally-oriented. So are so-called past and future.

*In other words, **when we focus upon ego** (when we focus upon so-called past and future) **our inner energetic template aligns horizontally, rather than vertically. So, our inner energy does not connect to either Heaven or Earth. We, our bodymind, is not a conduit that serves to connect Heaven to Earth. We are an incomplete circuit. We do not connect with soul** as the soul resides in a vertical position above the crown of the head. Ego-focus is directed toward, and creates, horizontal patterns of energy. Ego-focus limits us. It creates kinks (horizontal deviations) in our vertically-oriented Lines of Force. Which outwardly result in limitation. Limited health. Limited self-awareness. Limited success.*

Yet we can fly above the clouds . . .
To be vertical is to defeat the horizontal.

In fact, this is the only way
To eliminate confusion and limitation
For you cannot defeat these false illusions
Of the mind
By using mind
(Intellect)

APPLICATION OF

V   A
E   C
R   T
T   I
I   V
C   I
A   T
L   Y

THE RULES OF ENGAGEMENT OF VERTICAL ACTIVITY DETERMINE THE SCHEDULE AND PACE OF APPLICATION OF VERTICAL ACTIVITIES. FOLLOW THE CLASSICAL SEQUENCE EMPLOYED FOR HEALING (AND RESOLUTION OF ISSUES).

Efficient resolution (healing) of conflict, dysfunction, disease and other energetic stagnancy occurs in a specific sequence. Generally, first approach (resolve, heal) unresolved issues (resistance, blockage) of greatest *density*. Second, approach unresolved issues of progressively subtle *density*. In other words, this protocol typically prescribes body-based energywork (bodywork, exercise, yoga, etc.) to initially release densest energies, followed by mind work (psychenergetic therapy, psychotherapy, mental re-patterning, neurological re-patterning, etc.).

As an example, I worked with a client who has a fear of being trapped in elevators. As a kid she was in an elevator in a tall building in downtown Chicago with a friend of her father and his daughter. The father and daughter were playing around, and intentionally hit the "stop" button – after which the elevator traveled very slowly while the alarm sounded. My client was ten years old at the time, and quite frightened. Through the years, try as she might to acclimate to elevators, she maintained a tinge of fear during each ride. To heal (release) the fear, anxiety and worry, we developed a regimen by which she first worked her body (working out, intentional dance and other more specific methods) and then approached the cognitive mind – to gain understanding of the dynamics of her fear patterns, so she could ultimately release repetitive mental patterns, and comfortably ride elevators.

* * *

ANCILLARY CONCEPT

Density

What is density? Density has two common meanings when used in the context of bodymind energetics. One subjective meaning. One objective meaning. Density, from a **subjective** perspective, refers to a general sense of energetic quality. This ranges from weightlessness to heaviness, thinness to thickness, transparency (clarity) to opaqueness, etc. For example, what if you were to describe each of your friends as a song? Obviously each friend is different – so, one may be described as a happy song, another as a heavy song, another as a light song, another as a gloomy song, etc. These songs express the general sense of density of each person's essence (persona, aura). Density from an **objective** perspective, describes the inverse of energetic vibration (more specifically – the velocity of vibration) of a person, thing or event. In other words, the higher the velocity of the sum of an individual's energy – the lower the density. This is explained in Physics 101. The faster that quantum particles travel (vibrate) the greater the space in-between particles – hence, the lower the overall density, as there is more space between particles.

* * *

ALL WE NEED IS A CURSORY UNDERSTANDING OF (SUBJECTIVE) DENSITY – TO EXERCISE THE RULES OF ENGAGEMENT OF VERTICAL ACTIVITY (A/K/A CLASSICAL HEALING PROTOCOL). We simply need to understand that greatest blockage/resistance is of relatively great (subjective) density. In other words, relatively dense issues feel/seem/are of relatively "heavy", "thick" and/or "rigid" quality. This cursory understanding will help us to be in accord with classic healing protocol which prescribes that we first approach blockages of greatest density (by first dealing with the bodily aspect of the bodymind), and thereafter dealing with relatively subtle unresolved energetic patterns. For instance, symptoms/issues that feel more acute, need to be attended to first. Common sense, right? Mere restatement of the obvious . . . .

The vertical transcends the horizontal

VERTICALLY-ALIGNED THOUGHT, WORD AND ACTION HELP US TO DISSIPATE PHYSICAL, MENTAL, EMOTIONAL, AND SPIRITUAL IMBALANCES (STAGNANCIES) – HORIZONTAL PATTERNS OF STUCK ENERGY. There are two ways in which vertical-focus helps us to defeat horizontal patterns of dysfunction. Simply stated:

1)   Vertical-focus blocks (bypasses) and releases horizontal-focus (as they are mutually exclusive); and

2)   Vertical-focus taps the wisdom of the soul, Heaven and Earth (vertical energies that course through, and empower, the bodymind).

In sum
Vertical-focus serves two functions
To bypass (and release) the negativity of horizontal imbalance
And
To tap the positivity of the soul, Heaven and Earth.

FROM AN OBJECTIVE PERSPECTIVE, VERTICALLY-ALIGNED THOUGHT, WORD AND ACTION RAISE OUR INNER VIBRATION. Enhanced inner vibration lifts us from the bondage of horizontal resistance and blockage. Enhanced inner vibration helps to straighten kinks in the vertical Lines of Force that define our inner blueprint.

Chapter Four

INNER CREATES OUTER

Inner Landscape

Magnetically Attracts

(Creates)

Material Experience

"The different sensory stimuli to which [hu]man[s] react[s] –
Tactual, visual, gustatory, auditory, and olfactory –
Are produced by vibratory variations in electrons and protons.
The vibrations in turn are regulated by "lifetrons,"
Subtle life forces or finer-than-atomic energies
Intelligently charged
[By conscious intention, breath, and subconscious landscape]."
— Paramahansa Yogananda
Autobiography of a Yogi

AS WITHIN, SO WITHOUT. Our inner (energetic) template creates (magnetically attracts) our outer, worldly, material existence. We create our life experience. We are not victims of experience. We are the cause of our experiences. How can this be true? The Law of Attraction is the engine of life experience. Recall that the Law of Attraction is a magnet (electromagnetic mechanism) that attracts the *triggers* – in the form of (specific) people, objects and events that carry (specific) lessons that will help us to master needed unresolved life lessons – to facilitate evolution of our inner landscape, the core of who we are.

How does the Law of Attraction work? Its mechanics are quite simple. In succinct terms, the inner blueprint attracts life lessons to help us evolve.

The inner template exhibits weaknesses that mirror unresolved aspects of our mentality and emotionality. These weaknesses appear as kinks (non-vertical portions) in the Lines of Force of the Antahkarana (the vertical, central channel of energy that courses through us). Recall that our conscious and subconscious energies attract lessons. The unconscious aspect of psyche' attracts two-thirds of our material life experience; conscious patterns attract one-third of our material experience. Subconscious and conscious mind are pools of electromagnetic waveforms. Subconscious and conscious mind create our outer world . . . via the magnetic force of the Law of Attraction.

For example, the client with fear of elevators, described earlier, observed that she seemed to continually attract life experiences that forced her to deal with the emotion of fear. Only after years of vertical activity (vertical exercise, therapy, disciplined practice, thought, word and action) did her inner fear begin to subside. As a result of lessened conscious and subconscious fear, she no longer needed to repeat acute experiences of fear – to force her to deal with fear (and release psyche's attachment to the emotion of fear – and the energetic seed beneath the emotion of fear). In other words, she no longer needed to attract "triggers" in the form of people, objects and events, to cause her to experience the emotion of fear. Recall that to heal (resolve issues), one must re-experience the unresolved feeling (the wounded aspect), then release the egoic attachment, and connect to consciousness via the soul. We create our outer experience to facilitate inner resolution.

Nor can you achieve the pinnacle of success
Success aligned with the truth of your core being
By residing in the horizontal.

ALIGNED SUCCESS

Highest success is aligned with guidance by the soul. History observes that soul-inspired success is all that is remembered through the millennia. History does not recall the individual who earned great sums of wealth (with the exceptions of Bill Gates, Warren Buffet and others who use(d) their wealth for immense philanthropic purposes). Rather, history recalls the accomplishments of individuals such as Amadeus Mozart (music), Michelangelo (artist), Winston Churchill (skilled warrior, tactician and leader), and Mother Theresa (compassion). Certainly, none of the aforementioned individuals (except the philanthropic billionaires) are remembered due to the magnitude of their bank accounts. Yet, please note that anyone who is able to live each moment in love, as a loving being, adds as much to society and the universe as any of the aforementioned beings. As the highest achievement is love. In each moment.

Aligned success in its most potent form is love. A life spent loving others and oneself is to fly the highest spiritual path – regardless what form it may take. Aligned success for one may be honor as a great warrior (e.g., the courageous warriors who took Normandy during WWII to bring world peace), a life committed to motherhood, careers as janitor, teacher, architect, truck driver, piano-tuner, short-order cook, or whatever. Career path doesn't matter much – as long as one is connected to the inspiration of the soul in each moment. Remember that you are not what you do. You are who you are. **What you do is not who you are. You are a human being. Not a human doing. Yet, of course it is easiest to remain aligned with the soul (and to love in each moment) when career is aligned with core life purpose and life service.** If one participates at a job where they are forced to compromise their core truth – i.e., the job is not aligned with the wisdom of the soul – it is challenging to love in each moment. But, again, it is possible. It simply takes greater inner discipline.

Aligned success – success inspired by, and aligned with, the soul – is facilitated through vertical activity. It is easier to achieve aligned success when engaged in the practice of vertical activity (disciplined inner practice, thought, word and action). It is easier to achieve profound (aligned) success when focused in the vertical. It is improbable to reach the pinnacle of success when focused in the horizontal. Focus in the horizontal (so-called past and future, and the egoic aspect of personality) blocks us from our core life purpose and life service. And thereby keeps us from aligned success.

To be vertical
(aligned with soul)
Or to be horizontal?
The choice is ours
In each moment

THIS MOMENT: This moment is all there is. Countless poets have waxed on regarding "tomorrow never comes" (and so is imaginary). And (so-called) past is but an unreliable memory. So, all that is real . . . is now. And now. And now. This moment is all there is. This moment is all that is true. All that is reliable. This moment, too.

In theory, this moment connects you to all moments. All moments that occurred prior. All moments that will occur. Because everything is connected (as everything is energy), all moments are connected. To this moment. So, this moment influences all moments. Recall the example of the flapping of a hummingbird's wings in Japan that serves to influence the birth of a hurricane in the Azores. Similarly, this moment influences all moments. To the ancient Taoists, this moment defines the entirety of who you are. As does this moment. And this moment.

So, what you focus upon in this moment . . . matters. For this defines who you are. And defines the experiences that you attract. So, take responsibility. Choose wisely. Practice inner discipline to focus upon vertical waveforms (the seeds of vertical thought, word and action) in each moment, and practice vertical activity in each moment, to create the most beneficial and palatable life experience (from the perspective of the personality).

Chapter Five

INNER GEOMETRY

Gateway

To the Subconscious Mind

And

Soul-Alignment

(a/k/a Presence, Highest Inspiration

. . . & Profound Success)

INNER GEOMETRY REFERS TO THE NATURAL ALIGNMENT OF THE HUMAN FABRIC. Despite our external differences, every person is wired identically. Our energy systems are fundamentally indistinguishable.

Our bi-ped nature typifies the vertical-orientation of our natural inner geometric alignment. In fact, our very evolution took a quantum leap when we shifted from quadra-ped to bi-ped living. We gained speed of mobility, enhanced vertical reach, enhanced vision (as we viewed situations from a heightened vantage point), and longevity (due to advanced survival skills and as vertical posture favors the organic health of the bodymind – in spite of the effects of gravity upon the spine).

Recall that the subconscious mind attracts two-thirds of our material experience. If we can vertically align the geometry of the subconscious mind (good news – we can!), we significantly influence the quality of our material life. *The subconscious mind responds to specific patterns, shapes, symbols, and forms that stimulate visual, auditory, olfactory, gustatory, and kinesthetic sensory receptors. The stimuli may be incredibly subtle – yet with great effect upon the geometry of the subconscious mind.*

For example, Homeopathic remedies are nothing more than trace quantities of inert substances that significantly affect the health of the bodymind. Homeopathic remedies are not subject to approval by the Food and Drug Administration (FDA) as the amounts of active ingredients are so miniscule as to be scientifically indiscernible. *Yet, these etheric remedies substantially affect physical, emotional and spiritual health and well-being.*

> *Ever observe that*
> *We tend to yawn*
> *Within seconds after another person yawns?*
> *Why is this?*

HOW IS IT POSSIBLE THAT TRACE STIMULI CAN INSPIRE PROFOUND EFFECT UPON THE BODYMIND, INCLUDING THE SUBCONSCIOUS MIND? The answer to this crucial question is revealed through analysis from an energetic perspective. The answer is – because everything is made of energy – including both the bodymind and the Homeopathic agent. Everything in the universe influences every other thing in the universe. And again . . . recall the Japanese hummingbird and the African hurricane. In the specific case of Homeopathic remedies, the **energy** of the active ingredient, regardless how miniscule in quantity, affects the **energy** of the bodymind. Similarly, the subtlest pattern, shape, symbol, and visual, auditory, olfactory, gustatory and kinesthetic cues have the power to influence the subconscious aspect of the bodymind to an exponential degree. This causes exponential modification of our material life experience.

HOW TO USE VERTICAL ACTIVITY AND EXTERNAL SENSORY-STIMULATING SUPPLEMENTS TO INSPIRE SOUL-ALIGNMENT.

It takes time to enhance our inner verticality and, thus, to transform our lives. How much time? It is impossible to foresee. However, during the course of energywork practice I observed two trends.

INSTANTANEOUS RESOLUTION. First, I observed that healing (resolution of an issue) may occur in an instant. Some might describe this as a "miracle." Miracles occur if such result is in the highest interest of the evolution of the soul. For instance, there are numerous recorded cases of people experiencing Near-Death-Experiences. Why didn't they die, given similar circumstances in which countless others died? Could it be that it wasn't their "time?" In other words, could it be that they still had more lessons to learn while alive – so they were given more days? Although improbable, miracles are possible – and most certainly do occur on occasion.

THE NINETY-DAY RULE. Second, I observed that the natural law that stipulates that profound (substantial and lasting) transformation takes (approximately) ninety days at the minimum (in cases other than miracles) – seems to hold true in many instances. This is the Ninety-Day Rule. The mechanics of the Ninety-Day Rule are straightforward. **The "Shadow" aspect of the subconscious egoic personality rears its (oftentimes) "ugly" head, for the first time, at approximately ninety days into any (relatively close) interpersonal dynamic.** In other words, we expose "the other side" (unresolved aspects of personality) of who we are, for the first time, at approximately ninety days – to an unsuspecting lover, friend, employee, peer, acquaintance, etc. – and vice-versa. For example, have you ever observed that the initial three months of romantic relationship may seem almost blissful – yet, inevitably, at some juncture, you begin to see more of the personality of the other person – their (so-called) flaws – and they begin to see your flaws? This dance is explained at length in the book entitled *Conscious Relationship*. This typically occurs at ninety days into a relationship. And accompanies close relationships of any sort – romantic, work, familial, etc. *In this regard, it is helpful to apply external sensory-stimulating supplements for at least ninety days.*

"Psyche' requires rhythm for growth."
— Dr. Jack Miller
The Phoenix Project

REPETITION: The subconscious mind – the powerful inner magnet that attracts two-thirds of our material experience – requires repetition (of vertical activity) to evolve. The neural grooves of patterned dysfunction run deep. Like grooves in a 33 rpm record, our dysfunctional thoughts, words and actions continue to run the same track – until repetition of vertical activity causes the neural grooves to smooth, in favor of new, healthy neural grooves (*"positive habits"* in the form of appropriate thoughts, words and action). Repetition means daily practice (and in the instances of mindfulness and breath, moment-to-moment practice). *A tiny drop of vertical activity, applied on a daily basis, brings a pound of cure . . . Especially when practiced for at least ninety days.*

A great paradox.
Although action speaks more loudly than word
And word more loudly than thought
Intention
The silent creator
Is the foundation of all
And thereby most important

INTENTION (TURBO-CHARGES VERTICALITY). A friend who practices acupuncture told me that precise placement of a needle is less important than the intention to place the needle in the right spot. So, even if an acupuncture needle is placed a few millimeters away from the "sweet spot", its action will be perfect if the acupuncturist clearly intends to place the needle in the right spot. A more everyday (somewhat trite) example is the well-intended but inappropriately chosen gift – a person may give a gift with great intention, but the gift itself is not preferred by the receiver. Nonetheless, the clear intention of the giver brings great joy to the recipient, regardless how tacky (un-preferred) the gift. Sincere intention adds value to even the tackiest gift. *In this regard, it is of utmost urgency to practice vertical activity with clear intention – for only then will vertical activity be empowered to facilitate utmost evolution.*

Intention, body-centered breath, and repetition
Are the precursors
Of profound resolution, healing, and evolution.

Body-centered breath and repetition
Are the foundation
Of Soul-Aligned Activity.

Intention, body-centered breath and repetition
Bring us closer to the wisdom of the soul.

BODY-CENTERED BREATH (TURBO-CHARGES INTENTION).
Intention, repetition and breath are the precursors of profound
resolution, healing, and evolution. Intention is powerful. Clear
intention can over-ride potential dilution of healing capacity rendered
by an inappropriately placed acupuncture needle, and can over-ride
the possibility of hurt feelings rendered by an inappropriately chosen
gift. **Certainly, intention is powerful. Yet, body-centered breath is
equally important.**

The mechanics underlying the power of intention and breath are
similar. Recall that the intention of vertical activity is to strengthen
and align the Lines of Force (the central channel of energy that
courses from Heaven to Earth, and Earth to Heaven, via the
bodymind – which serves to plug us into the electromagnetic circuit
and wisdom of Heaven and Earth). The ultimate power of intention
lies in its ability to connect us to Heaven and Earth (via the soul).
Even if we practice vertical activity (thought, word and action) in an
inaccurate manner, clear intention can over-ride potential dilution of
verticality of the Lines of Force. In other words, clear intention to
align with soul, Heaven and Earth can over-power any obstacle or
misstep. Although it is theoretically simple to maintain clear intention
in any moment – in practice it is challenging to maintain clear
intention on a continuing moment-by-moment basis. Similar to
intention, focused breathing empowers verticality of inner geometry.

**How does focused breathing (body-centered breathwork) promote
present moment mindfulness? In summary, focused breathing
serves two functions. First, it defeats the meandering of the**

monkeymind (ego). Second, it serves to help us connect to the energy of Heaven and Earth.

SACRED GEOMETRIC SUPPLEMENTS. Sacred geometry refers to multi-sensory forms and symbology that innately *(automatically)* unlock the subconscious mind's stagnant patterns. How? Good question. Modern science has no answer to this question. Nor does ancient philosophy, per se. Yet, the Ancients were empiricists – they didn't require explanation, as long as something was practical (i.e., it worked). Unlike Western scientists, the Ancients accepted function regardless of whether or not they could explain why a protocol was effective. The Ancients observed that *focus* upon certain patterns, shapes, symbols, and forms – that stimulate visual, auditory, olfactory, gustatory, and kinesthetic sensory receptors – is somehow able to significantly influence the subconscious mind. External sensory-stimulating supplements supplement vertical activity to transform consciousness (at conscious and subconscious levels).

External sensory-stimulating supplements open numerous gateways of access to the wisdom of the soul. The sensory aspect of the nervous system presents five such gateways. Mathematically related, the visual, auditory, olfactory, gustatory, and kinesthetic sensory pathways provide entry to the innermost aspects of the brain and energetic systems – presenting access to the soul and core energetic systems (the Antahkarana).

"The Foundation of Vertical Activity" (focused intention, breath and repetition), Sensory Activity, and External Sensory-Stimulating Supplements (which innately influence the physical, emotional and spiritual systems of the bodymind) *are the tools that sculpt subconscious and conscious transformation.* Vertical activity is the foundation of life – and transformation. "The foundation of vertical activity" (mindfulness and breath) is a constant, moment-to-moment practice. External sensory-stimulating supplements are supplements that innately help us to unlock unresolved, buried subconscious and conscious physical, mental, emotional and spiritual patterns.

Chapter Six

3 TOOLS
ACTIVATE
SOUL-ALIGNMENT

Ancient Technology for Evolution and Success

1.   Foundation of Soul-Alignment
                (Mental focus upon Body-Centered Breathing)

2.   Sensory Activity
                (Creative Intention, Word & Action to activate
the 5 Senses)

3.   Sensory-Stimulating Supplements
                (External supplements to activate the 5 senses)

RECALL THAT external sensory-stimulating supplements are props employed in addition to a repetitive regimen of Sensory (creative) Activity, and the Foundation of Soul-Aligned Activity (a constant practice of present moment mindfulness including mental focus upon body-centered breath). External sensory-stimulating supplements are keys that further facilitate healing of the unresolved aspects of the subconscious template; like body-centered breathing, mindfulness and sensory activity, these supplements are a direct gateway/portal to the doors of the subconscious mind. These groupings of tools can help us remove blocks to self-awareness, higher consciousness and success. Each tool has a different mechanism, a unique function, and a distinct energetic vibration. The tools may be used concurrently or in any sequence you intuitively prefer.

All of the tools promote verticality of the inner template, aligning our inner geometry with the soul. **In technical terms, mindfulness, body-centered breathing, sensory activity, and external sensory-stimulating supplements help to straighten the Lines of Force of the Antahkarana.** They increase our energetic vibration. This serves to attract, via the mechanism of the Law of Attraction, higher vibration (i.e., more palatable – from the perspective of the egoic mind) people, objects and events to trigger lessons that promote self-awareness and, enhanced success. Call upon external sensory-stimulating supplements to support vertically-oriented thought, word, action and breath.

A Sequential Approach to Healing
Exponentially Enhances Efficiency:
Healing From Density to Subtlety

Let's consider the example of a river. Similar to the human bodymind, unimpeded river flow represents health, whereas stagnant flow leads to dysfunction and disease. Suppose a beaver builds a dam in an otherwise healthy, flowing river. Within moments, flow ceases. Within a few days, a scum clouds the surface of the water. Over time, surface scum thickens, blocking sunlight into the river. Oxygen supply is depleted, affecting sea life. Meanwhile, bottom mud and muck thicken, as river flow no longer carries loosened muck downstream. The water becomes de-oxygenated and saturated with muck and impurity (bacteria, etc.).

The primary question is . . . how do we restore the health and vitality of the river? Do we initially try to clean the water? Of course not. Obviously, the most effective and efficient action is to remove the beaver's dam.

Removal of the beaver dam represents initial healing of the greatest density of blockage. The dam is of greater relative density than the dirty water or muck in the river. By initially removing the dam, we restore health efficiently. Were we to initially try filtering the dirty water, we would obviously be wasting time and effort. Healing the bodymind and aura is similar. To heal most effectively and efficiently, we first heal greatest density, then approach increasingly subtle density (with regard to the cause of dysfunction and disease).

In sum, it is advisable to first employ physical movement of the body – to initiate a healing regimen. This serves to "move" the greatest density of blockage.

The 3 types of tools that activate soul-alignment approach the bodymind (including the aura) through various entrances. Relatively superficial tools initially affect the physical aspect of the bodymind. They move the body. By moving the body, we enhance circulation of the blood, release toxins, massage the internal organs and cells, and affect energy flow. Physically-oriented tools (like working out – especially cardiovascular activity – and yoga postures) are a great initial step toward resolving *any* issues. For example, consider how you feel after you workout. You feel great, right? Active physical activity, such as working out, helps us to alleviate blockages of greatest density. Other tools approach gateways that include the visual, auditory, olfactory, gustatory and kinesthetic sensory systems. These entrances serve as points of ingress for resolving relatively subtle aspects of the self. These tools utilize relatively subtle vibrational action to affect the subconscious and conscious aspects of the self.

THE GREAT QUESTION IS . . . WHICH TOOLS ARE BEST FOR YOU? How do we choose the best tools to help us evolve most efficiently and effectively? The answer is multi-faceted. Sorry! There are a few things to consider when choosing tools of soul-alignment (verticality). First, know that our energy, our state of consciousness, changes in each moment. Recall that our state of evolution is dependent upon factors including focus upon the present moment (you are what you focus upon – nothing more, nothing less), pre-disposition (via lineage genetics), intention, degree of disciplined self-awareness, degree of disciplined soul-aligned activity, etc. No two people are in exactly the same state of evolution. Nor do we remain in the same state of evolution from one moment to the next – as a direct reflection of our momentary focus. Each of us requires a unique set of tools to help us gain awareness, release blockages, evolve, and ultimately gain aligned success.

Don't be afraid to try *any* tools that you sense may be helpful. On the other hand, don't be too attached to any specific tool. A tool may help you in one moment, but not the next moment. Trust your intuition. This may be difficult at first. Trust that the voice of intuition will become increasingly clear as you engage this process.

OVERVIEW OF SOUL-ALIGNED ACTIVITY

Constant focus on intention of presence
And body-centered breathing
An eternal meditation
Is the essence of Being

The foundation of presence is soul-aligned activity
As the soul resides only in the present moment

Being is the foundation of conscious doing
Just as presence is the foundation of conscious activity

Practice vertical activity
In every moment
Constant, unwavering
For repetition is precursor of comprehensive success

Supplement Being
With conscious doing.
(Sensory activity
Coupled with
Sensory-stimulating supplements
Catalysts of transformation)

Focused mindfulness and breath are the foundation of presence. And so of Being. Focused intention and breath are the foundation of vertical activity. They serve as the radar of soul-aligned activity, bringing vision and direction to conscious doing (sensory activity – creativity – and sensory-stimulating supplements).

Consciously intend and employ focused breath in every waking moment. This is an eternal, inner discipline. As Bruce Kumar Frantzis told me late one evening in his home in Fairfax, California – should a student do nothing but learn how to focus on the breath (abdominal breathing) in each moment, their life will transform dramatically. Recall that repetition is a necessary ingredient of subconscious transformation (release and re-patterning).

"Right Action" is tantamount to soul-aligned activity. Recall that Tibetan Lama Arjia Rinpoche asks himself, in each moment, "What is right action (i.e., "what is the best activity – or non-activity – that I can do/be in this moment, for the sake of the totality of universal consciousness?"). This is the essence of vertical activity, "conscious being and doing." **Conscious intention of presence and mental focus upon body-centered breathing are the foundation of "conscious BEING." Vertical thought, word, and action centered upon sensory creativity, supplemented by external sensory-stimulating supplements are "conscious DOING."**

External sensory-stimulating supplements are simply supplements that facilitate connection to the soul (via the 5 senses). These tools are keys that somehow as–though–automatically unlock blockage (horizontal static) from the subconscious, and serve to align the subconscious with the guidance of the soul. In other words, external sensory-stimulating supplements innately serve to reverse the karmic cycle (release blockage created by our prior inappropriate decisions, words and actions).

OVERVIEW OF VERTICAL ACTIVITY: 5 FUNDAMENTAL TOOLS. There are five tools that create the foundation of evolution and profound success. These are breath, non-directed thought (a/k/a mindfulness, intention of presence, IN-tention), directed thought (OUT-tention), word and action.

I have a friend who ventured to India to deepen his meditation practice. He found (and was found by) a wonderful guru who taught him much about life and meditation. Upon arrival from his trek, he was excited to share a fundamental lesson. He explained that many great meditators ask themselves the fundamental question, "who am I?" before meditating. The question of core truth (including core life purpose and life service) was the fundamental conscious exploration of the meditative journey. Similarly, this question and intention, the intention of knowing the truth of who we are at the core, is the fundamental and initial intention of vertical activity.

The core objective of vertical activity is presence. To be in the now. To be in truth. To be in the soul experience. To be connected to the wisdom of the soul, Heaven and Earth. To be the true self. To know who we are at the core. To experience who we are at the core. In every moment. And thereby to love, serve and create . . . completely.

1) INWARD-DIRECTED THOUGHT (a/k/a mindfulness, intention of presence, IN-tention). Intention focused upon presence, truth, vertical alignment with the soul, is the key to presence, truth, vertical alignment, health, abundance and success. **Great meditators focus upon vertical intention in every moment.** Believe it or not, this is more challenging than the greatest physical or academic challenge. SIMPLY INTEND TO BE PRESENT IN EACH MOMENT. Paradoxically, a simple task – yet great challenge. For conscious intention is every moment. **Do your best, build up to progressively longer periods of focus on inwardly-focused intention of presence.** This will connect you to truth and align your energy systems with the guidance of the eternal wisdom of the soul. This is a fundamental key to ultimate health, abundance and comprehensive success.

* * *

ADVANCED CONCEPT

Crystalline Structure of Water
Is Influenced by Intention

The ability of our intention to modify the crystalline structure of water in the bodymind provides compelling physical evidence of the power of intention. Scientists have photographic proof illustrating how the structure of water molecules is affected by emotion and intention. Various books describe this research.

Two-thirds of the bodymind is water. This infers the ability of intention to transform the majority of our inner landscape and bodymind. Which magnetically attracts (creates) transcendent material life experience.

* * *

Breath is the bridge
To Consciousness
Connecting Bodymind
To Heaven and Earth

2) VERTICAL, BODY-CENTERED BREATH: This is also referred to as Intentional Breathwork or Conscious Breathwork. Bruce Kumar Frantzis, arguably a master of the Taoist energetic arts, is the adopted son of Liu Hung Shieh, a renowned Taoist master residing in the Shao Lin Temple outside Beijing, China. I was fortunate to spend time in Kumar's home with his lovely family. Kumar taught me the fundamental aspects of Dragon & Tiger Qi Gong. I earned certification to teach this energetic system under his tutelage. As I said before in the text, late one evening he told me that if I taught someone nothing more than Abdominal Breathing, and if they practiced this discipline with each waking breath, miraculous transformation would benefit the individual. I trusted this advice so implicitly that I personally practiced Abdominal Breathing for the next two years – in virtually every waking breath. I believe that the results were transformative, as Kumar suggested beforehand. I experienced enhanced grounding – connection to Earth energy – which I could clearly feel move up through the soles of my feet, up my legs, to the navel (as a tingling, warm, water-like sensation). And I felt a heightened sense of vitality, intuition, synchronicity and clarity of dreams – evidence of connection to consciousness and Heavenly energy. Although I learned numerous methods of conscious, body-centered breathwork, I found Abdominal Breathing, the simplest method, to be very effective. In total, I use four types of focused body-centered breathwork – namely, Abdominal-Breathing, Foot-Breathing, Heaven-and-Earth Breathing, and Emotional-Release Breathing.

The theory and practice of breathwork may sound a bit obscure. Overall, the physical air/oxygen (**Physical-Breath**) and energy-of-the-air (**Energy-Of-The-Breath**) may travel different courses through the bodymind. The physical process of breathing, via physical diaphragmatic movement, has a physical effect upon adjacent anatomy (known as **Anatomical-Expression-Of-The-Breath).**

We can direct the path of the **energy of the breath** by using mind's intention. *This is an immensely powerful process that has been recognized through the millennia as a pathway to accelerated consciousness.* Obviously, **physical breath**_travels the path of nose to lungs (inhalation) and back out the nose or mouth (exhalation). **Anatomical expression of the breath**, physical movement of anatomy apart from movement of the lungs due to diaphragmatic movement, influences the lower abdomen – causing the lower abdomen to rise and fall with each inhale and exhale, respectively.

In all types of body-centered breathwork, air physically flows into the lungs, via the nose, and flows back out the nose (or mouth).

ABDOMINAL-BREATHING – a simple technique (yet difficult – for this practice is every moment). Focus the mind's attention upon the Anatomical-Expression-Of-The-Breath, the natural rise and fall of the abdomen (approximately two inches below the navel), noting the anterior, posterior and lateral movement of the abdomen. Most effective practice involves moment-to-moment practice of Abdominal-Breathing. Again, simple . . . yet difficult. **Abdominal-Breathing defeats the scattered monkeymind by forcing the mind to focus in the body – which causes a shift from ego-focus to soul-focus.** Abdominal-Breathing inspires connection to both Heaven and Earth – bringing highest inspiration and grounding. **Try to use Abdominal-Breathing in every breath. I recommend mastery of Abdominal-Breathing before trying other methods of breathwork.** As Kumar said, given mastery of Abdominal-Breathing, unbridled evolution is possible.

FOOT-BREATHING (EARTH-BREATHING). This is an excellent technique for grounding. Foot breathing draws the energy of the Earth up into the body – electromagnetically grounding the electrical circuit that is the body. The intention of Foot-Breathing is to draw Earth energy up from the Earth Star, an energy center (a chakra, like a small sun) located approximately 24 inches beneath the feet, up through the balls of the feet, up the legs, to the Lower Tan Tien (Taoist description of the energy center located two inches beneath the navel in the center of the body), and then back down the legs, down through the heels of the feet, back down to the position of the Earth Star. I tend to visualize a tube of energy flowing up either one leg, or up both legs concurrently. I visualize the tubes as red, white or gold in color. Sometimes the color red sends more energy. Sometimes the other colors are more effective. Coordinate inhalation with uptake of energy from the Earth, and exhale when sending energy down from the Lower Tan Tien. You may feel a river of energy, tingling, and/or a sense of peace/serenity/rootedness/connection to self/slower thoughts when connected to the Earth via Foot-Breathing. Foot-Breathing is especially beneficial when feeling ungrounded (with worry, anxiety, confusion, lost feeling, etc.). Overall, focus the mind's intention upon movement of Earth energy up through the legs, to the groin, and back down to the Earth – whenever you'd like – but especially when feeling ungrounded.

HEAVEN-BREATH-EARTH-BREATH. Heaven-Breath-Earth-Breath is a hybrid of breathing techniques that I was taught in Qi Gong, Yoga and Meditation practice. This method combines Heaven-directed breathwork with Earth-Breathing. In Earth-Breathing, we focus upon bringing Earth energy up to the Lower Tan Tien (the Second Chakra), then sending the energy back to Earth. In Heaven-Breath, focus upon descension of the energy of Heaven into the Crown Chakra and all lower chakras, with inhalation. Then we exhale the energy of the breath back to Heaven. During Heaven-Breath, the mind's attention is upon the Third-Eye Chakra, Heart Chakra and Second Chakra. Then use one round of Earth Breath. Alternate rounds of Earth-Breath and Heaven-Breath. This is an advanced method. Please do not try this without first mastering the prior two methods, and without the instruction of an experienced Qi Gong (or yoga or meditation) teacher. I tend to do one Heaven Breath, followed by an Earth Breath, and so on.

CAUTION: Do not simply focus on Heaven-Breath without interspersed Earth-Breath. Be certain to focus upon the Lower Tan Tien (and Heart Chakra) during Heaven-Breathing. Arguably, it is dangerous to focus all attention in the head – in an ungrounded manner. Focus of energy solely in the cranial area may lead to physical, mental and emotional imbalance. Each of the above techniques are, essentially, aspects of Qi Gong practice (and yogic and meditative practice).

EMOTIONAL-RELEASE BREATHING. The concept of Emotional-Release Breathing is to release the energy underlying stuck emotion. When feeling "negative" emotion (negativity in the body) and "negative" thoughts, try to feel where the emotion is located in the body. This forces you to feel (not think). The theory is that the energy underlying the emotion is in the body where you "feel" the emotion. Inhale (intend) the energy-of-the-breath to move to the area of the emotion in the body. Visualize white energy, drawn in via the inhalation to the area; this serves to cleanse and dissolve the seed of energy underlying the stuck emotion. Then exhale the remnants of the stuck emotion (gray in color, etc.). This is best accomplished with a healing professional (Qi Gong Therapist, etc.).

Vertical Intention (to be Present) and Vertical Breath are the foundation of presence, self-knowledge, truth, and ascension. Vertical breath and intention create the platform for effective meditation.

3) OUTWARD-DIRECTED CONSCIOUS INTENTION (OUT-tention, vertical thought). "Vertical intention" (inward-directed intention, mindfulness, IN-tention, intention of presence) regards intent to be present, in the moment. Period. Outward-directed intention (OUT-tention) regards all other conscious thoughts that constitute "right action" in the moment. In other words, OUT-tention is thought focused on conscious, aligned material activity. Vertical IN-tention serves to promote vertical alignment of our inner energy landscape. Vertical OUT-tention serves focuses upon aligned creation in the material world. IN-tention (and breath) are the foundation for OUT-tention and worldly word and action.

4) VERTICAL WORD. The word. The word is powerful. More so than thought, as word takes the energy of thought and moves it outward into the world. Words are powerful as they tap the subconscious through three mechanisms. Namely, phonetics, tone, and implicit intent.

a) PHONETICS: Words are comprised of syllables that consist of consonants and vowels. In particular, uttered vowels affect the subconscious. The subconscious mind is programmed to respond to specific vowel sounds in specific ways. For example, the vowel sound "ahhh" is uplifting – i.e., it is interpreted by the subconscious mind as positive energy, vitalizing, restorative. This is why Sanskrit, an "empowered" language (more on this later), uses many "ahhh" sounds – notably in proper names. For example, the man who introduced yoga to the Western world is Paramahansa Yogananda (pronounced   Pah-rah-mah-hahn-sah   Yo-gah-nahn-dah)   –   an energetically vibrant name that innately invokes positivity into the subconscious landscape.

TONE: Words are uttered with tone. We can say the same word with varying volume, speed, inflection, resonance, and timbre (pitch). The specific pitch (tone) of an utterance influences the word's effect upon the energy systems of both speaker and listener.

* * *

ANCILLARY CONCEPT

**Relationship of Musical and Visual Vibrations
(Musical Notes and Visual Colors)**

Musical notes and visual colors are mirror-images, distinguished merely by (harmonic frequency) octave. Visual colors vibrate at a higher octave than musical notes. Ever notice that there are seven musical notes in a major scale, and seven colors in a rainbow? This is not a coincidence. The colors of the rainbow – red, orange, yellow, green, blue, indigo and violet – correspond to the musical notes C, D, E, F, G, A, B, respectively.

Every aspect of the bodymind responds to (i.e., is influenced by) vibration. Specific aspects of the bodymind (including the internal organs and chakra energy centers) respond to specific vibrational tones – presented visually (color), audibly (musical note), kinesthetically, aromatically (natural scents which are of distinct vibrations), and gustatorily (as natural spices are of distance vibrations). So, we may apply color, sound, movement, scent and flavor to resonate (heal) the bodymind (and auric field).

Specifically, the seven major chakras of the bodymind respond to distinct harmonic tones as follows. The Root Chakra responds to the note "C", the Sacral Chakra responds to "D", the Solar Plexus Chakra responds to "E", the Heart Chakra responds to "F", the Throat Chakra responds to "G", the Third Eye responds to "A", and the Crown Chakra responds to "B."

Visual stimuli work in the same way as auditory stimuli. For example, the Root Chakra responds to the color red; Sacral Chakra responds to orange; Solar Plexus Chakra responds to yellow; Heart Chakra responds to green (and pink); Throat Chakra responds to light-medium blue; Third-Eye Chakra responds to indigo; and Crown Chakra responds to violet.

* * *

b) INTENT. Words are powerful. Words, like underlying intention, are binary. They either align us with soul, or block our true path. Use words responsibly. Try not to harm others with words. Should you not heed this suggestion, recall that karmic law justly causes any harm that we inflict upon others to return tenfold – as a helpful lesson (to teach us how to use words more responsibly). Know this. Be pro-actively responsible with words – as they help us sculpt material experience.

5) SOUL-ALIGNED ACTION: Vertical action, tantamount to soul-aligned activity, is profound creativity (and love). Action directly creates real-time, material life experience. Action is binary. Conscious activity aligns us with the vertical posture of the soul. Inconscious activity blocks the guidance of the wisdom of the soul.

Core creativity expresses as visual art, sound, and kinesthetic movement (dance or solo athleticism). Ala the artist, musician and dancer (or athlete). Action based in core creativity, from the soul, begets enhanced soul alignment (verticality). Action based in egoic confusion, begets further confusion.

Don't act simply to act. **Act only when clearly grounded in your truth, and aligned with the wisdom of the soul.** *Otherwise, action is not merely* *potentially futile but worse yet, may undermine verticality. The dualistic world is binary (by definition). An action is either helpful or harmful (with regard to well-being). An action either feeds the soul, or feeds the ego.*

Each of us is born an artist, musician or dancer (athlete). This innate condition is either supported or suppressed by our parents and environment. This condition (artistry) is sourced by soul. Artistry, in turn, feeds the soul. Visual art and sonic art are mathematically related. Art, music and dance draw energies of Heaven and Earth to us – although in varying degree. They connect us to highest inspiration, and to grounding.

Creativity serves two fundamental purposes. First, creativity serves to facilitate release of blocked energy (including emotion and thoughts) in the bodymind. For purposes of releasing energy, employ a natural sequence of healing – which specifies first releasing densest blockage and, thereafter, subtle blockage. Initially apply creative pursuits that release greatest energy. This includes physically-active creative endeavors. As an example, start with dance/movement, then introduce music, then consider sculpting and creation of visual art. Even if you were to somehow create dance, music and art simultaneously – dance likely would have greatest initial impact, then music, then visual art; this parallels healing protocol that first releases density, and thereafter subtle (energetic) blockage and resistance.

Second, creativity serves to connect us to Highest Inspiration (Natural Order, God, etc.). To connect to Highest Inspiration, apply whatever form of creativity speaks from the deepest aspect of self. This may be easiest once densest blockages have been moved, through application of an initial sequence of initial dance, etc. For example, if you observed that you were more interested in creating music than dance or art as a child – create music to tap Highest Inspiration. This may serve to integrate a connection to soul-consciousness on its own accord. If not, it might be helpful to initially move densest blockages using another mode of creativity (i.e., movement).

LINEAGE OF ARTISTIC INSPIRATION

Visual art is sourced by Heaven
And the touch of Earth
And so lifts the mind to soaring heights
Sustaining bodily flow

Sonic art is inspired by both Heaven and Earth
And so impassions both body and mind in unison
A transcendent bodymind experience

Dance is inspired by Earth
But also the touch of Heaven
And so releases the body to ecstasy
Opening mental flow

Visual art, sonic art and dance are each sourced by different relative amounts of Heaven energy and Earth energy, respectively. And, as no two humans create art in the same way, everyone innately calls upon varied amounts of the energies of Heaven and Earth while engaged in artistic endeavors. This subtle degree of variance is succinctly explained by the mechanics and physiology of the eyes, ears and body.

The eyes are extraordinarily sensitive and complex instruments. The eyes are able to sense and, coupled with the brain, interpret high frequency information (visual stimuli). Visual energy (information) is of higher frequency than sonic information. Physiologically, the mechanism of seeing requires an extraordinary amount of brain capacity and brain function. The mechanism of seeing, of sensing and interpreting high-frequency visual energy, uses relatively more brain power (and relatively less body power) than either hearing or dancing.

The mechanism of hearing, the auricular canal, is responsible for both hearing and bodily balance. This suggests that sonic interpretation is influenced by both sonic sensitivity and body-based factors.

The mechanism of dance is predominantly body-based. Yet affects the brain/mind in two ways. First, dance moves the brain, its chemistry, the cranial organs of the endocrine system, its vasculature, the bodymind, etc. Second, dance influences the emotions – which are stored in the body. Release of stagnant emotional energy positively influences thought processes (a reverse feedback loop). For example, do you observe that your thoughts (interpretation of events, decision-making, etc.) are more clear following dance or intense athleticism?

In summary, vision is relatively mind-based (brain-based) relative to hearing (both mind and body-based) and dance (predominantly body-based). Why is this important information? How does this information affect our everyday lives? Because the relationship of the senses of sight, hearing and movement suggests how we might most effectively and efficiently resolve issues (and heal).

However, please receive this information with more than a grain of salt. As everyone processes artistic endeavor differently. The sequence presented below is a general reference, but certainly not a strict guideline. Each of us is born with different fundamental life lessons to learn. And each of us processes, expresses and employs artistic expression in different ways, and for different reasons.

RESOLUTION OF ENERGY
THROUGH ART, MUSIC AND DANCE

To resolve the unresolved
Ascend the Lineage of Artistic Inspiration
(i.e., reverse the lineage)
As profound healing
Initially approaches density (of body)
And only thereafter subtlety (of mind)

Begin with dance
Release stagnancy trapped in the body
And again know what it is to feel
Then may music carry you to bodily-integration of truth
And thereafter may visual art impart illumination

The suggested sequence posed herein is not a strict guideline. Yet, it may serve as a point of reference, a starting point – for efficient and effective resolution (healing) of issues that block us from highest alignment.

The sequence of energetic resolution (and healing) using artistic means is straightforward. Recall that healing always takes place from resolution of density to subtlety. So, to efficiently and effectively resolve energetic conflict (heal), simply reverse the Lineage of Artistic Inspiration. Initially, resolve lower-frequency, relatively dense information, and thereafter resolve higher-frequency, relatively subtle information.

In simplest terms, start with the body. Move the body. Shake everything loose (literally). Dance, dance, dance. Dance when you awaken. Dance before you sleep. Dance to celebrate being alive. Dance whatever emotion you are feeling in the moment. Or dance to stay alive. Or play (transcendent solo) sport intensely, etc. Sweat. Burn. Move. Express. Focus on emotion while moving. Breathe. Intend. Move it out. Then . . . crank the music. Mozart, old Led Zeppelin, Bob Marley, Miles Davis, Stevie Ray Vaughn, Ray Charles, Aretha Franklin. It doesn't matter. But play music that moves you to the core. Play music that makes you move – even if you aren't in an appropriate forum in which to move outwardly – *move inwardly*. Feel your heart open. Feel Heaven and Earth. Feel the heaviness of your feet, rooted to the Earth. Feel breath open. Feed your soul. Integrate truth in your body. And then . . . finally, open your eyes to the beauty of finest visual art (whatever that may be to you). Illuminate the soul. See as you've never seen before. Envision the infinite. Let it guide you.

The core of vertical action is visual art, musical art and kinesthetic art. Recall that each of us is born an artist, musician and/or dancer. These activities are born in the soul, feed the soul, and align us with the soul. The love that fuels artistic capacities is the foundation of all inspired action.

Like any thought, word or action, artwork may be sourced by either the soul or the egoic aspect of the personality. Artwork – like thought, word and action – is binary. It is soul-aligned or not (i.e., ego-aligned). It is vertical or horizontal, respectively. **To assure verticality of artwork, soul-alignment, be certain to exercise intention and**

body-centered breath. Focus upon IN-tention (of presence) – mindfulness rooted in the present moment. Breathe. Focus your attention upon expression of the breath in the body. [See the description of "Abdominal Breathing" and other methods.] INtention and breath focused upon the body (especially focused on the Lower Tan Tien – as practiced in Abdominal Breathing) exponentially enhances the probability of creation of soul-aligned art. Remember, the ego (egoic personality) is a great trickster. Without conscious focus of intention and breath, ego may source any artistic expression.

a) SOUL-BASED (VERTICAL) VISUAL ART. Visual art inspired by the soul may be rooted in intuition and/or technique. Visual art may be two-dimensional or three-dimensional (sculpture). Visual art unlocks stagnant subconscious patterns, and innately reprograms consciousness through subconscious influence – re-patterning of inner geometry. As described earlier in the text, each primary color, sacred visual shape, form and symbol profoundly influences energetic centers and internal organ systems.

Two powerful techniques help to kick-start resolution of subconscious patterns. First, create visual art using your non-dominant hand. This subverts habitually-oriented (profane, lower mind-sourced) artistry, opening the gateway to more intuitive, less programmed, creation. For instance, if you're a lefty, draw with your right hand. Second, focus upon what you *feel* as you create – rather than upon what you think. Highest inspiration flows parallel to feelings – not thoughts. For example, if you feel angry/sad/fearful/worried/joyous prior to lifting brush to pallet, continue to feel the emotion/s – don't suppress emotion when engaged in artistic creation. Certainly you've observed that the finest art can move us to tears, laughter and limitless other emotional states – in an instant. Conversely, finest art is created in alignment with the soul – and emotions. And so affects the soul and emotions of all who view the artwork.

To optimize the probability of soul-aligned artistry, be certain to focus your intention and breath upon the present moment.

b) SOUL-BASED (VERTICAL) MUSICAL ART (SOUND). Like vertical art and dance, music sourced by the soul may be rooted in intuition and/or technique. Great works of music are frequently described in literature using the adjectives "heavenly" and "grounding." These descriptions are accurate – as greatest music derives from the soul, and balanced connection to Heaven and Earth.

To maximize the probability of soul-based (rather than ego-based) musical creation, maintain focus of intention and breath upon the breath's expression in the lower abdomen – Abdominal Breathing (and other body-centered breathing techniques). This helps to promote presence (present moment mindfulness), which inspires soul-based creation.

Unlike visual art, wherein creation uses a brush and a pallet of color (clay or other media), musical art – other than voice – requires use of a relatively-complex instrument. Each musical instrument draws upon, and creates, a distinct vibration – that affects the musician and listeners. The manner in which an instrument is played (with hands, feet and/or breath), the materials of an instrument (metal, wood and/or other materials), and the octave of sound an instrument creates, have an effect upon how the instrument affects the inner geometry of the subconscious and conscious aspects of the mind of musician and listener.

Some instruments are played using the breath and hands (woodwinds like flute, saxophone, clarinet, and oboe), some simply use the hands (piano, guitar, violin, drums, percussion), some employ hands and feet (contemporary drum kit and percussion). Obviously the mind must devote its attention to the anatomical aspect of the body that plays the instrument – this affects the musician, the music created and, subsequently, the listener.

Instruments are crafted of wood, metal, skins (drums), plastics, other materials, and combinations of materials. Each material influences the vibration of the music created by the instrument, and affects both listener and musician.

Instruments create specific musical notes in various octaves. Low octave tones move dense energy. Higher frequency sound moves relatively subtle energy. A specific musical note played in any octave affects one specific internal organ (and chakra). As lower octave tones move densest energy, a specific musical note played in a low octave moves densest energy from a specific internal organ (and chakra). The same musical note played in a higher octave releases relatively subtle energy from the same internal organ (and chakra). For example, the musical tone "C" affects the Root Chakra. The "C" tone played in a low octave moves dense energy from the Root Chakra. The "C" tone played in a relatively higher octave moves subtle energy from the Root Chakra.

Large (deep-pitched) drums and percussion instruments are said to most obviously draw up the energy (vertical waveforms) of the Earth. Many ancient cultures used drums in healing ceremonies – to generate healing grounding energy. Consistent with healing protocol (initially heal density and thereafter heal subtle energy dysfunction), the Ancients used deep-pitched drums as a first line of defense (first step) to heal people afflicted with disease (physical and emotional). I often used deep-pitched drums, or a large gong, early in healing sessions to supplement bodywork and energywork methods. Later in the session it might be appropriate to use higher-pitched cymbals or other higher-pitched percussion instruments to move relatively subtle energy blockages.

Sound affects the subconscious by employing phonetic and toning keys that re-pattern and re-program the subconscious mind. This is described in detail, later in this section.

To optimize the probability of creation of soul-aligned sound, be certain to focus your intention and breath upon the present moment (by focusing the mind's attention upon expression of the breath in the body).

c) SOUL-ALIGNED (VERTICAL) KINESTHETIC ART (MOVEMENT, DANCE).

Like vertical art and music, dance (athleticism) sourced by the soul may be rooted in intuition and/or technique. Greatest dance (and athleticism) derives from connection to the soul, Heaven and Earth. Dance connects us to Earth more obviously than either visual art or music – as the act of dance *demands* contact with the surface of the Earth.

To maximize the probability of soul-based (rather than ego-based) dance and athletic expression, maintain focus of intention and breath upon the breath's expression in the lower abdomen – Abdominal Breathing. This automatically serves to promote presence (present moment mindfulness) – and defeats the scattering meandering of the monkeymind.

Unlike visual art, which often uses a brush and a pallet of color (or clay or other media), and unlike musical art – which typically uses relatively-complex instruments – dance is relatively primordial – requiring no props whatsoever. This simplistic format, combined with Earth-connection (grounding), activates **the great power of dance (movement) as an initial step in the process of resolution (healing) of the subconscious energy template.**

d) INTENTION AND BREATH. If we intend to align with the soul, we shall. Recall the acupuncturist of honorable healing intention who misplaces a needle by a few millimeters. The treatment is still effective in spite of technical flaw, *as intention is more powerful than technique.* Focus on body-based expression of the breath empowers intention, mindfulness, and soul-aligned creation.

SACRED GEOMETRIC SUPPLEMENTS: 6 SENSORY KEYS UNLOCK THE SUBCONSCIOUS MIND. *The six senses are gateways to the subconscious mind.* Vision, hearing, smell, taste, movement, and sixth-sense, extrasensory perception, provide entry into the recesses of the subconscious mind. Why is this important? How does this affect our daily lives? Recall that the subconscious aspect of the mind magnetically creates (attracts) two-thirds of our life experience. So, it is IMPORTANT to know how to influence the subconscious mind so you can influence your material life experience. Otherwise you create by default.

1) VISUAL KEYS UNLOCK THE SUBCONSCIOUS MIND. Visual shapes (symbols) and colors influence the subconscious mind. Shapes (symbols) and colors unlock pre-patterned neural grooves that are deeply embedded in subconscious programming (from childhood or, from an Eastern perspective, from the spillage of karma). Specific shapes (symbols) open distinct sectors of the subconscious and conscious bodymind, as do specific colors. Through the millennia, ancient cultures noted the empirical effects of sacred visual forms and colors upon human function.

a)   SACRED SHAPE (SYMBOLOGY)

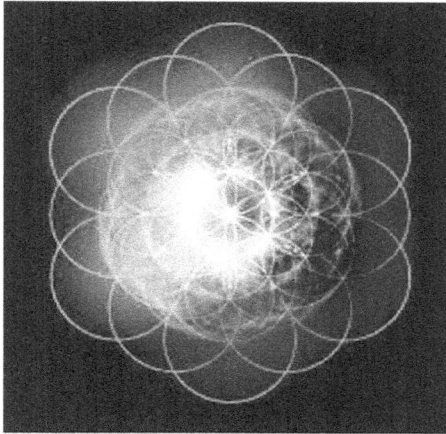

Sacred shapes unlock dysfunctional patterns buried deep in psyche'. Sacred shapes also vitalize the subconscious aspect of the personality – inspiring soul-aligned resolution of the inner energetic blueprint.

Fundamental shapes found in nature are derived from circles rather than straight lines and ninety-degree angles (which are human creations). Squares, rectangles and triangles do not naturally occur in nature. Through the millennia, a handful of shapes are described as the foundation of universal symbols. These shapes include ↑, ∨, +, ○, and △.

A circle ○ represents completion (of a process or cycle). An equilateral triangle △, although not a prehistoric symbol (as not found in early rock carvings or cave paintings), primarily represents the holy, the divine, and the holy number three – which symbolizes a holy trinity (and power, warning). A square, when positioned in a horizontal-vertical position, represents the two dimensions that comprise a surface. So, a square ☐ represents ground, land, Earth. A cross with equal-length arms + represents various phenomena, including sun and weather. A dot, or very small, filled circle, is seen in cave paintings and ancient rock carvings. Some paintings used dots arranged in spiral patterns. Dots seem to refer to phenomena that are small or of short duration. Straight vertical lines represent unity, oneness, the true self, the Infinite, and a bridge from lower to higher dimensions.

The preceding description of a few symbols barely scratches the surface of symbology. Yet, the point is that the subconscious mind understands symbols. We can influence subconscious patterns and programming by employing the ancient technology of symbology.

How do we use symbols to facilitate our transformation? Simply focus upon or visualize the symbols (in etheric or written form, respectively) – while engaging life. Meanwhile, we intend presence and focus on body-centered breath. Believe it or not, this profoundly affects our inner geometry, aligning it with the soul. Certain symbols may intuitively appeal to you. Others may not. A specific symbol may appeal to you in one moment and not the next moment. Trust your intuition.

SOUL-ALIGNED LANGUAGE (ALPHABETS). There are five symbolically-empowered (and phonetically empowered) languages/ alphabets. These are Aramaic, Tibetan, Chinese, Sanskrit and Hebrew. In theory, these language systems employ cutting-edge ancient symbolic and phonetic technologies to innately inspire advancement of any society that chose to use these languages. **These languages utilize sacred shapes throughout their written form, and sacred phonetics throughout their spoken form – to turbo-charge the power of written and spoken word. The thought was that anyone who wrote, read, spoke or listened to these languages would benefit from languages' direct effects upon the subconscious template.** They felt that their written and spoken words promoted accelerated evolution for entire societies.

How can we utilize the technology of sacred alphabets? Explore. **Research. You may find that certain ancient, empowered languages/alphabets appeal to you. Feel free to focus upon specific empowered words, either in written or spoken form, which you feel may help you generally, or to face a specific challenge.**

b) SACRED COLOR

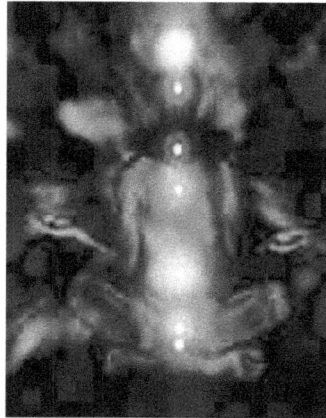

Sacred Color and the Chakras

As described earlier in the text, specific colors affect our major energy centers (chakras) and internal organ systems. The seven colors of the rainbow affect the seven major chakras – the sequence ranging from red to violet affects the chakra range from Root Chakra to Crown Chakra, respectively. The internal organs are affected in the following specific sequence. Red affects the Heart organ (not chakra) – red facilitates release of impatience and intolerance from the heart organ; yellow affects Spleen, Pancreas and Stomach – releases worry; green affects the Liver and Gallbladder – releases anger; blue affects the Kidneys – releases fear; and white affects the Lungs – releases sadness and sorrow.

How can we utilize the technology of sacred color? While engaged in life situations, feeling emotion (or not), focus on the color that corresponds to the issue facing you – while intending presence and focused upon body-centered expression of the breath. For example, if feeling fearful, focus on the color blue (with your inner eye), which helps the kidneys to release fear, meanwhile turbo-charging release by consciously breathing and intending present moment mindfulness. Further, you might focus on the second chakra, for this is the region in which the kidneys reside – focus upon the color orange to heal the second chakra. This serves to release stuck emotional patterns of fear from the subconscious mind.

2) AUDITORY KEYS UNLOCK THE SUBCONSCIOUS MIND.

Sacred sounds influence the subconscious mind. These sounds unlock pre-patterned neural grooves deeply embedded in subconscious programming (from childhood and preceding adult experience or, from an Eastern perspective, from the spillage of karma). Specific phonetic pronunciations influence distinct sectors of the subconscious, as do specific musical tones. Through the millennia, ancient cultures observed and noted the empirical effects of sacred phonetics and tone upon human function.

Sacred Sound

a) **PHONETICS**: The phonetic sounds of distinct syllables and groupings of syllables affect the subconscious mind. The energy centers, internal organs and other cellular aspects of the bodymind respond to vowel sounds and consonant sounds. As mentioned prior, the (East) Indians (Hindus) believe that the vowel sound "ahhh" has a positive effect upon the subconscious template. For example, as mentioned earlier, parents may give their children positively-charged names such as Paramahansa Yogananda – a name comprised of repetitive "ahhh" sounds (he introduced yoga to the USA). As another example, the highest mantra (a repetitive prayer spoken aloud or inwardly) of the Hindu faith is the Gayatri Mantra – which also utilizes repetitive "ahhh" vowel sounds (Om Buhr Om Buvaha, Om Swaha, Om Maha, Om Janaha, Om Tapaha, Om Satya, etc.) This is a blessing of each chakra – releasing negativity from, and drawing positive energy to, each energy center.

In Taoist (Chinese) philosophy, the belief is that the kidneys (which hold fear) respond to the vowel sound "oh." The spleen, pancreas and stomach (worry) respond to the vowel sound "oo" (as in flute). The heart (impatience and intolerance) responds to the vowel sound "ahhh." The liver and gallbladder (anger) respond to the consonant sound "shhh." The lungs (sadness and sorrow) respond to the consonant sound "sss."

b) MANTRA (REPETITIVE PHONETIC PRAYER): Hindu faith utilizes repetitive prayer, as do many other religions (Muslim, Christian, and others). For example, the Gayatri Mantra, mentioned above, may be **repeated silently or aloud to bring positive energy to the subconscious template** and bodymind. Many devotees of Hindu tradition carry a bracelet or necklace of 108 beads and, like using Rosary beads, repeat a prayer 108 times, using the beads to count the number of repetitions. Repetitive prayer has great cumulative effect upon subconscious programming – tantamount to reprogramming. Another example of mantra regards Transcendental Meditation ("TM"). A few years ago I attended a lecture by renowned film-maker David Lynch. He assembled a non-profit organization, funded by a book he recently wrote, which funds Transcendental Meditation for children in school. TM exercises repetitive inward focus upon a "secret" word that is given to students by a guru.

c) TONING (CHAKRAS AND INTERNAL ORGANS): As mentioned earlier in this text, specific musical notes affect the chakra energetic centers and internal organs. The sequence of musical notes "C" through "G" affects the Solar Plexus Chakra through Throat Chakra, respectively; the Third-Eye is affected by the musical note A; and the Crown Chakra is affected by the musical note B. In other words, we apply "A" to the Third-Eye Chakra, and moving vertically apply "B" to the Crown Chakra, then begin at the Root Chakra (apply "C") and move vertically through the next successive chakras, applying "D" through "G."

As an example, during energywork sessions (tablework) it was not uncommon for clients to hear inner musical tones. I grabbed a guitar to determine the specific musical note that the individual heard. This illustrates how the Infinite sends innate healing vibrations to us – to help us resolve and heal our inner landscape. I observed that the musical note corresponded either to a specific chakra and/or internal organ that was most in need of energetic release and re-vitalization.

* * *

ADVANCED CONCEPT

Summary of the Healing Effect
Of Color and Phonetics
Upon Internal Organs and Emotions

In summary, the totality of the bodymind complex – including the subconscious mind, conscious mind, and aura – is affected by color, tone and phonetics [in addition to infinite other factors – most notably mindfulness (intention of presence) and conscious, body-centered breathing]. Specific subsystems of the bodymind – the chakra energy centers, internal organ systems, and emotions – are directly affected by color, tone and phonetics. The healing effect of color and tone upon the chakra energy system is described earlier. The healing effects of color, tone and phonetics upon the internal organ system follows. Of course, this is most powerful when coupled with mindfulness (intention of presence) and conscious, body-centered breathing.

The Kidneys (which hold fear) are positively affected by the color Indigo, and phonetic vowel sound "Wo." Heart (which holds impatience and intolerance) is affected by the color Red, and the phonetic vowel sound "Hah." Spleen, Pancreas and Stomach (which hold worry) are affected by the color Yellow, and phonetic vowel sound "Hoo" – like "who"). Liver and Gallbladder (which hold anger) are affected by the color Green, and phonetic consonant sound "Shhh." And Lungs (which hold sadness and sorrow) are affected by the color White, and phonetic consonant sound "Sss."

Organ	Emotion	Color	Phonetic
Kidneys	Fear	Indigo	Wo
Heart	Impatience and Intolerance	Red	Hah
Spleen, Stomach, Pancreas	Worry	Yellow	Hoo
Liver, Gallbladder	Anger	Green	Shhh
Lungs	Sadness and Sorrow	White	Ssss

For example, to help facilitate release of a feeling of overwhelming sadness, first intend presence, and focus upon expression of the breath in the body. Then focus on the color white inwardly (e.g., as a brilliant white star) or outwardly – for as long as feels appropriate. Hear or sing the appropriate musical tone. Say the sound "sss" with each exhalation. You might inhale an image of the color of brilliant white. Experiment. There is a reason these techniques have been around for thousands of years. But, be certain to turbo-charge the process by using IN-tention (mindfulness, presence) and OUT-tention (specifically intend healing of sadness), and focus on body-centered breathing (such as Abdominal Breathing).

* * *

3) OLFACTORY KEYS UNLOCK THE SUBCONSCIOUS MIND.

Sacred (Soul-Aligned) Scent

While I was in college, a professor of Neuroanatomy had us perform an exercise in which we were instructed to close our eyes for three minutes and imagine the smell of burning leaves. To reduce the effects of air pollution, state laws regarding burning leaves had been changed since we were kids – no longer was it legal to burn leaves. Due to this change in the law, the professor presumed that we had not smelled burning leaves since childhood. After three minutes of visualization most students recalled vivid details of childhood associated with the smell of burning leaves. I was able to visualize a pile of leaves on the driveway in front of our home. I could smell the smoke. I sensed it was a crisp, cloudy autumn day in Chicago. It felt like mid-afternoon. And I sensed that I was approximately eight years of age at the time. A vivid memory unlocked by memory of scent.

The point of the exercise was to gain firsthand observation of the power of the connection between smell and long-term memory (through the brain's Amygdala, a primordial aspect of the nervous system). Sense of smell immediately connects us to a core aspect of the subconscious mind. Memory of the smell of burning leaves served to reveal buried childhood memories from classmates and myself. As the teacher planned, this provided strong evidence of the power of the olfactory sense's connection to the subconscious mind.

Why is this important in our everyday lives? Recall that the subconscious mind creates (magnetically attracts) two-thirds of our life experience. So, sacred (soul-aligned) scent is another means by which we can positively influence the subconscious landscape and, thereby, our dynamics of the people, objects and events that we experience in everyday living.

SOUL-ALIGNED SCENT: AROMATHERAPY (ESSENTIAL OILS THERAPY)

A popular example of a sacred scent that can open gateways to repattern the subconscious mind is Aromatherapy agents. Aromatherapy refers to essential (aroma-producing) oils that are extracted from plants and flowers to treat dysfunction. Essential oils are extracted from roots, stalks, bark, rind, leaves and flowers of a plant. Essential oils are combined with another substance (typically oil, lotion or alcohol). They are inhaled, applied topically on the skin, and non-topically sprayed into the air. In combination with oil they are effective agents for therapeutic massage, and effective bath oils. Contemporary practice of aromatherapy was introduced in Europe in the early 1900s.

The physiology of aromatherapy acts via nerves in the nose to influence the endocrine and enzyme systems in the body. The fragrances stimulate nerve impulses that influence subconscious memory and emotion. Aromatherapy agents may stimulate or relax the bodymind, depending upon the source plant's natural characteristics.

Aromatherapy elixirs align our energy with the guidance of the soul, inspiration of Heaven and Earth, and help us release stagnant energy from the subconscious mind.

* * *

ANCILLARY CONCEPT

Traditional Chinese Medicine
and the Holistic Nature of the Bodymind

It seems appropriate to present a cursory overview of a few aspects of Traditional Chinese Medicine (TCM) – which includes Acupuncture, Herbal Medicine, and Energy Medicine (a/k/a Vibrational Medicine, Qi Gong) – as this healing system provides evidence of holistic (unified) nature of the bodymind. I refer to the Chinese (Taoist) system only because I am somewhat familiar with this system – and ignorant regarding other equally beneficial systems of healing from around the world.

The ancient Taoists believed that the hands, feet, and ears are an exact (micro) template of the human body. Each provides a precise functional map of the body. In other words, manipulation of specific aspects of feet, hands or ears physiologically manipulates the corresponding aspect of the bodymind. For example, the big toe represents the cranium/brain. Manipulation of the big toe physiologically (energetically) manipulates the cranium/brain. Similarly, the cranium/brain can be manipulated by manipulating precise regions of the hands, the ears and, as aforementioned, the feet. "Reflexology" is a widely-known practice in which the peripheral anatomy may be manipulated to promote wellness in the body and mind.

TCM uses the tongue and pulses in the wrists for systemic diagnosis. This suggests that the tongue and wrists are connected to all bodymind function. The body and mind (and aura) are holistic. They are unified.

* * *

4) GUSTATORY KEYS UNLOCK THE SUBCONSCIOUS MIND.

a) SOUL-ALIGNED (VERTICAL) TASTE. Admittedly, my exposure to, and understanding of, energetic aspects of taste is limited. Yet, I am certain there is much research and theory on the topic, certainly of Taoist (Chinese) origin rooted in Traditional Chinese Medicine (TCM)

– as the tongue is an important diagnostic tool in TCM. Diagnosis utilizing the tongue considers the color, texture, size and other aspects of the tongue. This suggests that the tongue, and its connection to taste, is somehow connected to all aspects of the bodymind – including the subconscious mind. IN-tend, breathe . . . taste.

* * *

Additionally, although outside the scope of my limited understanding, different foods (including spices) affect the bodymind in profound ways. Many books describe the holistic, healing power of food. Foods affect our physiology, emotions, energetics and spiritual connection. Eat consciously. Intend presence. Breathe.

* * *

"You are what you eat."

— Anonymous

Yet, more so, you are what you intend.

b) SOUL-ALIGNED NUTRITION. You are what you eat. Yet, more so, you are what you focus upon in each moment. Do you recall this Taoist belief? The body physically recycles most of its cells every seven to ten years (although not the cerebral cortex or DNA). What we eat and, more so, the cumulative effect of our intention in each moment (over the past seven to ten years), and yet mostly, our intention in this moment, are the building blocks of the new bodymind. It is important to select foods that enhance our physical stature and inner (subconscious) template. Many books describe the vibrational (vertical) value (i.e., overall holistic benefit) of various foods. Nutritional value should consider physical, emotional and spiritual benefit of any food. For example, symptoms of loss of hair (baldness) may be treated (not necessarily cured) by eliminating beef, chicken and sugar from the diet (while combined with exercise to enhance blood flow).

c) SOUL-ALIGNED FOOD PREPARATION. Recall that the intention of an Acupuncturist trumps her technique. Similarly, intention to prepare a "healthy" meal is at least as important as proper preparation of the ingredients. Although certain religious tradition calls for a blessing over a meal once a meal has been prepared, it is equally important to maintain positive intention (soul focus) while preparing a meal.

For example, as cliché' as this may sound, while I resided at Esalen Institute (Big Sur, California) in a tipi in a garden overlooking the Pacific Ocean, I worked as a laborer in the five-acre garden/farm. I enjoyed this work and benefited greatly as I was reminded of the elements that help to create food. Plants require sun, rain, earth, labor and seed. So, while preparing a meal, or before I sat to eat a meal, I would visualize all the elements that created the meal (for example, a stalk of broccoli), and thank each of the five fundamental elements. Not only did this help to ground my intention for nutritional benefit before eating a meal, it also helped to modify the nutritional value of the food (again, as the water and other elements of the broccoli stalk, for instance, are physically influenced by intention).

Recall the aforementioned description of the effect of intention upon the crystalline structure of water molecules. Intended holistic nutritional value influences food quality that, in turn, influences the subconscious template.

Nutrients (vitamins, minerals, amino acids and fatty acids) and non-nutrient bioactive compounds (herbs, enzymes, probiotics, etc.) can help treatment of various diseases and dysfunctions. At the physical level, they influence chemical levels, hormonal balance, immune function, oxidation, genetic expression, blood health and levels of toxicity. At the etheric level, they influence the energy of the inner landscape and resultant life experience.

d) HYDRATION (WATER). Two-thirds of the body's composition is water (by weight). The bodymind is essentially a river. Blood circulation throughout the body serves to feed and cleanse the body. Health is flow. Death and disease occur when flow is restricted or blocked. The energies underlying disease, dysfunction, stagnant thoughts and stagnant emotion are water-soluble. Maintain a constant flow of water throughout the body to assist release of the matter and energy of disease and dysfunction. Drink at least two liters of pure water daily. Turbo-charge the effectiveness of hydration by employing mindfulness (vertical intention) while drinking water.

Recall that intention influences the crystalline structure of water molecules. Exercise conscious, body-centered breathing between sips.

5) KINESTHETIC KEYS UNLOCK THE SUBCONSCIOUS MIND.

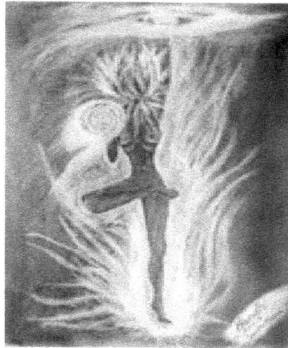

Sacred Dance and Athleticism move densest Energy

"Blood follows Energy"
– Traditional Chinese Medicine

Healing Protocol
Always flows
From healing densest blockage
To healing subtle resistance.
This infers the healing power
Of a sequence of healing
That prescribes bodily movement
As our first line of defense
To heal densest unresolved energies.

SOUL-ALIGNED MOVEMENT: The most effective and efficient healing protocol always approaches densest energetic (physical, mental and emotional) blockage first, and thereafter approaches progressively subtle blockage and resistance. Movement releases densest energy. ***Vertical movement (dance and athleticism) is our***

first line of defense when faced with unresolved conflict, disease, or dysfunction.

Why do we prefer to use soul-aligned movement (creation of dance or athleticism) as a first-line of defense versus disease, dysfunction and inner conflict – rather than creation of visual art or music? When faced with extreme, <u>dense</u> blockage, we are described as "not in the body" – out of touch with the core self (and bodymind). More specifically, primarily we are not in touch with grounding energy, the energy of the Earth. Secondarily, we are not in touch with the energy of Heaven. We've lost connection to the true (aligned) self. To clear densest energy first, connect to Earth via dance and movement. Recall that vertical (conscious) dance is sourced more by Earth than by Heaven – relative to creation of music (relatively equal sourcing by Heaven and Earth), and creation of visual art (sourced relatively more by Heaven than by Earth). Again, this sequence for healing is not set in stone – it's a matter of what works best for each of us. **Moving the body is the quickest and most powerful way to initially release densest blockage and resistance (to promote alignment with the wisdom and energy of the soul).**

VERTICAL DANCE, YOGA, QI GONG, SPORT, AND BODYWORK. Turbo-charge the healing power of dance, athleticism, yoga, qi gong, sport and bodywork with mindfulness (intend presence) and conscious focus upon expression of the breath in the body.

6) ETHERIC KEYS UNLOCK THE SUBCONSCIOUS MIND.

"When you pray
God listens
When you meditate
God speaks"

— Anonymous

a) VERTICAL PRAYER. Harvard Medical School conducted a study of the effectiveness of prayer. The conclusion of the double-blind study is that – more often than not – prayer works. The scientists did not attempt to explain the mechanism underlying prayer. Yet, prayer can be effective or relatively ineffective. The following suggestions enhance the efficiency and effectiveness of the power of prayer:

Four factors enhance the efficiency and effectiveness of Prayer:

1) Mindfulness (Focus upon the present moment);

2) Conscious Breathing (Focus upon bodily expression of breath);

3) Clear Intention (regarding your request / prayer; know what you want – yet ask for it to physically manifest only if it is aligned with the will of the Infinite (natural order); and

4) Non-Attachment. Ask, then let go of the desired outcome. Again, if aligned with the will of the Infinite, the wish will come true. If not, something better awaits. . . .

"Ask and ye shall receive."
— The Bible

"[Yet be] careful what you ask for

As you just might receive it."

— Anonymous

When we pray, the Infinite (highest inspiration, natural order) receives our request, statement or plea. So, it is of utmost importance to be certain that we ask for an outcome that is aligned with what is truly best for us – at the core of our being, the soul. . . . To accomplish this, pray for manifestation of what you desire – but only if this desire is aligned with the truth of your soul and the will of the Infinite (i.e., if the desire serves the best interest of your soul's evolution in the long-run).

To inspire soul-aligned prayer, use mindfulness (intention of presence) and focus upon bodily expression of aligned breathing (e.g., Abdominal Breathing, etc.). If we don't align with soul, we may ask for an outcome that serves the ego, rather than soul – which promotes short-term gratification but not lasting evolution and resultant material success.

All Soul-Aligned (Vertical) Tools are Precursors
To Stillness Meditation
As Meditation IS Verticality

"Be vertical . . . dissolve."

— Chris H.

"Meditation is
25% Willingness
25% Surrender
And 50% Grace"

— The Meditator Who Prefers To Remain Anonymous

We do not meditate.
We are meditated
By grace.
We simply create the possibility,

The platform,
For meditation
To grace us.

b) MEDITATION IS SOUL-ALIGNED (VERTICAL, BY DEFINITION).

Meditation

Noun. Emptying or concentration of mind: the emptying of the mind of thoughts, or the concentration of the mind on one thing, in order to aid mental or spiritual development, contemplation, or relaxation. Origin: 1175–1225; < Latin meditātiōn- (stem of meditātiō) a thinking over; replacing Middle English meditacioun < Anglo-French < Latin, as above.

The traditional (western-based) definition of "meditation" (above) is vague and subjective. Yet, meditation is an objective science . . . as objective as adding numbers . . . and as tangible as the Law of Gravity. The Western-based perspective of meditation is confused – because meditation is birthed in an Eastern-based paradigm of philosophy – which seems illogical or, at least, unintelligible, using Western-based reasoning. This is due, in part, to disparate definitions of "intelligence" by the conflictive paradigms. In the West, intelligence is logical use of the analytical mind, based upon a plausible phenomenological explanation. In the East, "intelligence" is holistic – intelligence focuses upon discovery of solutions that benefit mind, body and *spirit* – over the long-run. Easterners consider the soul, the spirit, to be a natural part of who we are – and a necessary consideration in any equation. **Western philosophy believes that answers are sourced by the brain. Easterners believe that answers are sourced by a universal source of omniscient, omnipresent information – that may be tapped through faculties other than analytical thinking and logic. The Eastern paradigm values meditation as the most efficient and effective bridge to an infinite**

pool of universal, omniscient, omnipresent information, vitality, and possibility.

Seven factors enhance the efficiency and effectiveness of Stillness Meditation:

1) Vertical Movement (Dance, Athleticism) (and, possibly, sonic creation, visual creation, and other forms of Vertical Activity) – before sitting;

2) Mindfulness (Intention of presence);

3) Copnscious Breathing (Focus on body-centered breath);

4) Listen with open mind and open heart (without agenda);

5) Willingness;

6) Surrender; and

7) Grace.

TURBO-CHARGE MEDITATION BY EMPLOYING MINDFULNESS (INTENTION OF PRESENCE) AND CONSCIOUS BREATHING. External sensory-stimulating supplements help us to innately (as though automatically) gain focus upon the present moment. Presence is a necessary precursor of effective meditation (i.e., connection to Highest Inspiration / Natural Order). Focus upon body-centered breath (by focusing on movement of the body that results as an expression of the breath – for example, focus upon the rise and fall of the lowest abdomen when we inhale/exhale) to gain presence. Mindfulness and conscious breathing turbo-charge the depth, efficiency and effectiveness of meditation.

c) **HOMEOPATHY:** Homeopathic remedies are etheric keys that help to unlock blockages in the bodymind, including the subconscious mind. Homeopathy was discovered in the 1800s by a German physician. The active ingredients in homeopathic remedies are trace amounts of inert materials the cause subtle energetic healing crises in specific aspects of the bodymind. For example, suppose an individual exhibits symptoms of a sore throat and inability to communicate in front of crowds. The theory is that if the homeopathic remedy appropriate for those symptoms was prescribed to a healthy person (without those symptoms), the healthy person would theoretically exhibit a (hint of) a sore throat and discomfort communicating to a crowd. In effect, homeopathic remedy subtly exacerbates symptomology in a person exhibiting symptoms – which sparks a subtle, typically undetectable energetic healing crisis. This passes quickly and brings healing.

As with all other (soul-aligned, vertical) activities, turbo-charge homeopathic remedies by supplementing their prescription with mindfulness, body-centered breathing, and specific intention.

d) FLOWER ESSENCES: Like homeopathic remedies, flower essences work ethereally to help the bodymind heal. Flower essences are comprised not even of trace amounts of physical substance but, rather, simply the energetic substance (essence) of flowers. Flower essences do not (necessarily) cause healing crises. Rather, they simply use the (etheric) intelligence of flowers to promote healing at an energetic level – which causes healing of the bodymind's physical, emotional, and spiritual aspects. As with all other (vertical) activities, turbo-charge flower essences by supplementing their prescription with mindfulness (INtention), body-centered breathing, and OUT-tention (outwardly-directed intention for a desired outcome).

e) BATHS: Baths help release toxins from the bodymind by dissipating toxins ("solute") through use of an "osmotic gradient." An osmotic gradient is a mechanism by which density in one solution is drawn into another solution, cleaning the initial solution. In other words, the salt in the bath water attracts bodily toxins (lactic acid, etc.) to leave the body (which holds a greater relative concentration of water) – so the toxins run "downhill" – from greater aqueous concentration (in the body) to lower aqueous concentration (in the salt-infused bathwater). Add a pint of salt (Epson Salt or Sea Salt) into a hot bath. For added benefit, add aromatherapy and herbs into the bathwater. A personal favorite is to create a Ginger Bath. Grate two ginger roots into pulp. Add the pulp into a near-boiling, large pot, let cook for five minutes, then strain the ginger broth into a hot bath, with or without salt. Sit for twenty minutes. The ginger acts as a natural antibiotic – and is somewhat effective at reversing symptoms of the common cold and other conditions.

As with all other (soul-aligned) activities, turbo-charge baths with mindfulness (INtention) and body-centered breathing [and specific intention of a desired outcome (OUT-tention), if applicable].

f) ENERGY WORK: Energywork is body-centered and/or ethereally-centered therapeutic practice that (when applied appropriately) tonifies the bodymind and releases stagnant energy from the bodymind. Energywork may be available through hospitals, MD-based clinics, Chiropractic offices, Massage Therapists, Spas, and other venues. If uncomfortable with a practitioner, walk away (immediately).

You are not who you think you are
You are who you feel you are
Your true self can only be felt
Not imagined or rationalized

7) SELF-AWARENESS HELPS UNLOCK THE SUBCONSCIOUS MIND (AND BODYMIND). Self-awareness is of utmost importance. For without self-awareness we are not inspired to practice soul-aligned activity at all – as our attention is focused in the ego, causing us to lead lives that don't feel genuine or aligned with the core truth. Self-awareness is of great practical importance. Without self-awareness, without knowing our true core life purpose and life service, without knowing how to truly love another being, and without knowing other aspects of the core self, we venture through life misguided – and do not create a life aligned with our core truth or *comprehensive* material success.

What is self-awareness? Understanding all nuances of the self. Its components. Its tendencies. Its likes. Its dislikes. Its strengths. Its weaknesses. Its inherent development. Its potential. Its limitations. Its core purpose. Its core service. Why is it important to be self-aware? So we lead lives that are aligned with the truth of who we are. So we are comfortable, excited, passionate, in harmony, and at peace with our lives. So we fulfill our life purpose, life service and attain material success. The following list describes aspects of self-awareness:

EMOTIONAL RELEASE HAS BOTH A BODY AND MIND COMPONENT. Release emotion, body's response to thought, from the body. Understand and re-pattern judgmental thought patterns. Vertical activity facilitates both processes.

RECALL THAT EMOTION IS THE BODY'S RESPONSE TO THOUGHT. Judgmental, unevolved thoughts (a/k/a non-accepting, stagnant, negative thoughts) trigger a sequence that stimulates the endocrine (hormonal) system to send specific hormones to attach to receptor sites on specific internal organs. This causes stagnant (negative) energy to be stored in the body – in the form of stagnant (negative) emotions. Recall that anger is stored (stuck) in the liver; fear in the kidneys; worry in the spleen, pancreas and stomach; impatience and intolerance in the heart; and sadness and sorrow are stuck in the lungs. Healing takes place from healing densest blockage to healing progressively subtle issues. By moving the body (kinesthetic activity), we can initiate the process of releasing negativity (stuck emotion) from the body.

•   **EMOTIONAL RELEASE WORK FOCUSES UPON RELEASE OF STUCK EMOTION AND NEGATIVITY FROM THE BODY.** Intention of presence, body-centered breathing, and sensory activity (including self-observation and awareness of the emotions and thought patterns) serve to inspire release of stuck emotion and bodily negativity.

UNDERSTAND, REVEAL, FEEL, IDENTIFY AND RELEASE STUCK EMOTION FROM THE BODY. Stagnant emotion blocks the flow of our lives. To resolve emotion, we must **re-experience the original feeling** that was buried deep in the subconscious mind. To do so, we magnetically attract people, objects and events that trigger us to again feel the original feeling. To heal – we must reveal (the original feeling), feel, and release the stuck emotion. INtention and focus on expression of body-centered breath facilitate this process.

UNDERSTAND THE NINETY-DAY RULE AND ITS INTERPERSONAL DYNAMICS. It takes approximately ninety days (at a minimum) to establish trust at a subconscious level, to see deeper truth when faced with new situations. The shadow aspect of the personality (the ego) reveals itself in interpersonal dynamics at approximately ninety days. This occurs in romantic relationship, friendship, the workplace, family life, and in any other relatively continual, close (relatively intimate) circumstance. Hint – move slowly and quietly until the passage of ninety days, at which time you will observe a very different dynamic than originally presented upon first meeting. [This is described in detail in the book entitled *Conscious Relationship*.]

UNDERSTAND THE NATURE OF RELATIONSHIP. The purpose of relationship is to help us evolve – by exposing us to lessons presented through interpersonal dynamics with other people (and/or groups of people). Relationship is like a Venus Flytrap plant. A Venus Flytrap plant has beautiful, aromatic nectar that lures prey into the center of the plant. Once the prey is well within the center of the plant, the hidden jaws of the plant snap shut, trapping the prey.
The nectar of the plant symbolizes the perceived value of the other person (as examples – beauty in the case of romantic relationship; reliability, trust, joy and serenity in the case of valued friendship; and purpose, service security and respect in the case of workplace). The initial days of interpersonal dynamics typically seem pleasant. It is the nectar of the other person (or group of people) that keeps us engaged in relationship with the individual(s). But, at approximately ninety days the shadow aspect of the egoic personality – both ours and theirs – reveal themselves for the first time. Not atypically, we are shocked to learn that the person *whom we thought we knew so well* (ha!) has "another side" to their personality. Don't be surprised. Rather, anticipate this. We all have unresolved ego/shadow issues in the initial phases of our personal evolution (process of self-

awareness). Be aware that **you attracted the other individual(s) to act as (a) mirror(s) of your own unresolved issues – so you can clearly see yourself, and release your own unresolved emotional/mental stagnancy. Relationship is a great reflecting pool. A forum for self-evolution – through dynamic with another. The positive aspects of relationship – beauty, friendship, companionship, material benefits – are secondary.**

IDENTIFY AND PERFORM CORE LIFE PURPOSE. Our core purpose is to express our core creativity. Ancient philosophies describe this as **"giving back to Source" (i.e., we create art, music, or dance to honor the Infinite through highest inspiration).** Each of us is born an artist, musician or dancer (athlete) – which is either suppressed or supported by the environment. **Life purpose is known eternally to the soul. To help identify life purpose, align with the soul** using INtention (mindfulness, intention of presence), body-centered breathing, OUT-tention and Vertical Activity augmented with External sensory-stimulating supplements.

IDENTIFY AND PERFORM CORE LIFE SERVICE. Core service is always known to the soul. Align with soul using intention, breath and vertical activity to identify life service. Serve wholeheartedly. The Earth and its inhabitants need help!!! Thank you.

RECOGNIZE AND UNDERSTAND UNION OF LIFE PURPOSE AND LIFE SERVICE. With the passing of time, the activity of life purpose and life service may merge. This is neither better nor worse than if life purpose and life service remain separate types of activity. Yet, I have observed individuals whose life purpose and life service somehow seemed to eventually merge into a single activity. If nothing else, this causes efficiency of effort. The advantage to merger of life purpose and life service is that life purpose, by definition, is one's passion. Thereby, *service becomes not merely a heart-felt joy due to being able to help someone – but becomes a greater joy as the activity is a preferred passion.* So, merging of life purpose and life service is a gift!

For example, I am a musician by birth. I have played guitar since I was eight years old. Through adolescence I loved playing guitar and singing, especially with my brother, a great guitarist. In my twenties, I enjoyed writing music and lyrics. I recorded quite a bit of music, mostly rock music. In my thirties I became interested in jazz and Eastern-based music. I then learned to play sitar. I was blessed to form a trio with Mr. Ed Ludwig, an excellent tabla player who also plays rock and jazz on a drum kit, and Mr. Nathan Swanson, an exemplary violinist/viola-ist/cellist/mandolinist. We create CDs that combine Eastern and Western musical sensibilities. Recently I began chanting on our CDs. So, now the music is a meditation. For us. And an audience. The music now serves the public in a healing and educational capacity – much like this book and energywork – my life service. So, my core life purpose now also fulfills an aspect of life service. A joy!!!

UNDERSTAND THE DIFFERENCE BETWEEN, AND ATTAIN, HAPPINESS, JOY AND BLISS. Happiness, joy and bliss are distinct states of awareness. There is more to a profoundly successful life than mere happiness. Joy and bliss are equally vital aspects of success. Happiness is material fulfillment that satisfies the desires of the egoic personality and aligned personality (as long as the materiality is aligned with guidance of the soul). Joy is soul fulfillment – typically attained through service to others. Bliss is transcendent – satisfaction of the "oversoul" (connection to the Infinite).

DIFFERENTIATE WORKING SMART VERSUS WORKING HARD. Soul guidance leads us to vocational and avocational positions aligned with our life purpose and/or life service. Working smart is working in a capacity aligned with soul. **Purposeful service doesn't feel like work – as it taps passion – which actually brings us vitalizing energy**; it vitalizes us, rather than "drains" us.

Be aware that **the type of work we do, as long as not harmful to others or the environment, doesn't matter – as long as we are present, connected to our truth (love) in every moment. Yet, it is easier to be present when focused upon work that is aligned with core truth.** Working hard infers toiling when not present – not mindful, as the chore at hand is not aligned with core truth (and may override attempts to be present).

UNDERSTAND ENLIGHTENMENT. Enlightenment does not occur in the so-called future. **Enlightenment is now. Enlightenment is, quite simply, absolute presence. Absolute focus in the present**

moment. Absolute connection to the soul. The foundation of presence is built upon INtention (intention of presence), supported by body-centered breathing, and Vertical Activity (including emotional release work), supplemented by External sensory-stimulating supplements. Enlightenment is synonymous with presence and self-awareness. We are absolutely present when absolutely self-aware.

USE VERTICAL GATEWAYS TO OPEN THE SUBCONSCIOUS MIND (AND BODYMIND). Open soul-aligned gateways of health, evolution, and comprehensive material success by utilizing the ancient technologies of guided language, sound (tone and phonetics), visual cues (symbology and color), kinesthetic movement (self and administered), smell, taste, creativity, emotional release, prayer and meditation. Turbo-charge these practices by using INtention (intention of presence) and body-centered breathing.

PROACTIVELY ATTRACT SOUL GUIDANCE IN THE FORM OF SYNCHRONICITY, INTUITION, DREAMS . . . AND MIRACLES. We create our life experience by magnetically-attracting necessary life lessons (to help us evolve). When present, aligned with soul, the soul provides hints, some subtle and some not-so-subtle, in the form of intuition, dreams, synchronicity . . . and miracles. Use this technology to help guide you to core truth and aligned success.

RECOGNIZE FORESEEABLE AGES OF TRANSITION. The human fabric is subject to foreseeable changes at approximate intervals of linear time.

1) NINETY-DAY RULE. As described above, it takes approximately ninety days to establish trust (at an energetic level). Relationships frequently "transform" at approximately ninety days, as the hidden (shadow) aspect of the personality (ego) begins to reveal itself (from a subconscious level). Be aware that we all have a shadow aspect that reveals itself slowly – so know that it takes time to get to know someone (especially regarding their emotions and emotional reactiveness) – and vice-versa.

2) ENHANCED DEPTH OF INSIGHT EVERY 7 YEARS. Our inner energetic blueprint undergoes fundamental and pervasive shifts every seven years. This reflects shifts that take place in each major energy center (chakra). The technical mechanism is not important to understand. What is important is to understand are the stages of the energetic life cycle, which inspire chronological patterns of inner development (which create outer experience).

Foreseeable patterns of development generally reflect the following sequence. Until the onset of teen-age years, we develop physically, emotionally and mentally. From Years 14 to 21, we primarily develop emotionally. Recall that the endocrine system transcribes thought into emotion (as emotion is the body's response to thought). Certainly we have all observed that hormones are raging wildly during the teenage years – years of great emotional transformation. Consider the difference in the emotional maturity of a typical 14-year old (freshman in high school) as compared to a 21-year old (college graduate). Ages 22 – 28 are years of intellectual evolution. These are the years during which we hone our intellectual skills, either in the workplace or in graduate school.

The first of two profound life transformations occurs at age 28. Although a superficial glance might suggest that this is simply a time of growth into adulthood (enhanced material responsibility), we undergo tremendous internal transformation at this time. The mechanism, in general terms, is straight-forward. Simply, **at approximately age 28 the soul begins to reveal a bit more of itself than in prior years.** For the first quarter (or so) of life, the omniscient, omnipresent soul sits quietly, allowing the personality to do its thing (experiment, discover, evolve). But, at approximately age 28, **where the personality's thoughts, words and actions are not in alignment with the wisdom of the soul, great turbulence occurs.** In other words, we attract challenging life situations (triggers) to help us evolve, but unlike before, at a turbo-charged rate to help quicken our evolution (i.e., alignment with soul). If you're older than 28, recall ages 27 to 29. Did you undergo profound life change? If not, did your friends undergo dramatic change in life situations? I did. I changed career paths and let go of an engagement at age 28. My personality's preferred career plan and fiancee' were not right for me. (Nor was I right for her.) And my soul let me know (by turbo-charging the transformation). The transition wasn't much fun, nor was it graceful. But, nonetheless, my soul helped propel me closer to my truth.

Further evolutionary changes occur from ages 35 to 42, during which our evolution is similarly accelerated by freshly revealed, enhanced depth of soul. **However, if we still aren't on target with our life purpose and life service (aligned with soul) by age 42, quite often we get our butts kicked (from the perspective of the ego). This is a great gift from the soul and natural order (the Infinite) – for this is the big boost (mega-turbo-boost) that helps us find our truth. At age 42, if unaligned with core truth, we attract people, objects and events that rock our world – to help us let go of stagnant patterns that block us from core truth. For our own good.** Typically not much fun. But exceptionally helpful to our personal evolution. Further shifts occur at ages 56, 63, etc. (patterns of 7 and 14-year cycles). Observe these patterns. Recall patterns in your life. Observe these patterns in others. Understand that life shall bring profound shifts – for good reasons. Accept these shifts as they are helpful gifts!

1) REPETITION OF UNRESOLVED LIFE LESSONS EVERY 12 YEARS. Objectively observe life experience. We repeat patterns. Unresolved essential lessons repeat every twelve years.

In summary, it takes approximately ninety days (at a minimum) to develop trust (and see deeper truth) in new situations. We experience enhanced depth of insight every 7 years. We experience repetition of unresolved life lessons every twelve years. [The underlying mechanisms of these patterns are described in detail in *Encyclopedia of the Tao: A-to-Z* by this author.]

UNDERSTAND AND PRACTICE DAILY STILLNESS MEDITATION. Meditation is 25 percent willingness, 25 percent surrender and 50 percent grace. We *do not meditate. Rather, we are meditated (by grace). Intend. Breathe. Dissolve.*

It matters not what you do for a living, per se.
What matters
Is to live in the present moment
And to love in each moment.

Yet it is easier to be present
And to love
When in alignment
With your true life purpose
And life service
This is self-alignment
Soul-alignment

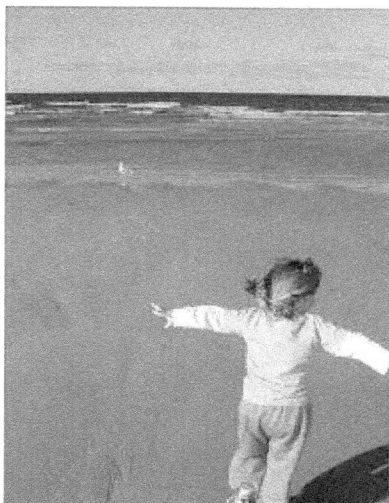

In this way self-awareness
And self-alignment
Help us
To know aligned happiness
To live the rapture of joy
To transcend in the ecstasy of bliss

So as to be the present moment

And to be love

Happiness, Joy and Bliss
Signs
That
Personality
Is
Aligned
With
Soul

DISSOLVE IN GRACE

Effortless
Miraculous
Love
Light
Consciousness and Material Success
Are Available
In Every Moment
To She Who Practices
Vertical Intention,
Vertical Breath
And Vertical Activity
A Soul-Aligned Being
[A Human Being, Not a Human Doing]
Creates
Profound
Material
Success
So Just Be

A 90-DAY
PROGRAM
OF
SOUL-ALIGNMENT
(VERTICALITY)

Ancient Technology
For
Evolution And Success

THE INHERENT VALUE of a ninety-day program of transformation is derived from various sources. First, any soul-aligned (vertical) activity, of its own accord, is a beneficial practice from the perspective of the soul. Second, repetition is powerful. Especially for ninety days pursuant to the precepts of the Ninety-Day Rule (as profound subconscious transformation is said to take ninety days at the minimum). Finally, the hope is that you will continue the newly acquired structure beyond ninety days – in the form of a lifelong practice that carries you to profound personal transformation and comprehensive success.

The purpose of the ninety-day practice is to enhance your inner energetic template, which causes natural acceleration of personal evolution and resultant success – transcribed as happiness, joy and bliss.

The structure and schedule of the program is flexible as contemporary life demands much time and energy. Should you decide to make this ninety-day practice a priority, you will benefit a hundred-fold relative to the investment of time and effort exacted of you.

The methods employed herein have withstood the test of time. The essential aspects of the program, mindfulness and body-centered breathing, the foundations of verticality have been used for many millennia. By millions of people. There is a reason for such longevity and popularity.

You design your ninety-day program. The main requirements are straightforward. First, observe practice for ninety continuous days. Second, observe the cadence of healing – first approach densest blockage of flow, then work toward resolving relative subtle resistance. (Start with physical movement, then other aspects of Vertical Activity as supplemented by External sensory-stimulating supplements, practiced upon a moment-to-moment exercise of present moment mindfulness and body-centered breathing. Observe. Be Aware. Evolve. Succeed in alignment with core truth as specified by the soul through enhanced intuition, dreams, synchronicity and … if aligned with the will of the Infinite, miracles.

Menu

TOOLBOX OF SACRED GEOMETRIC ACTIVITY & SUPPLEMENTS

Vertical (Soul-Aligned) Intention for Presence (Mindfulness)

Vertical Breath
> Abdominal Breath (Qi Gong)
> Foot-Breath (Qi Gong)
> Fire-Water-Ice Emotional Release Breath (Qi Gong)
> Fire Breath (Yoga)

Vertical Activity
> Vertical Vision
> Symbology
> Color

Vertical Sound
> Phonetics (Mantra)
> Tone

Vertical Scent
> Aromatherapy

Vertical Taste & Nutrition
> Food Preparation
> Hydration

Vertical Movement (Dance & Athleticism)
> Dance, Yoga, Qi Gong, Sport, Bodywork

Vertical Etheric Activity
> Prayer
> Stillness Meditation
> Homeopathy
> Flower Essences
> Baths
> EnergyWork
> Self-Awareness

Itinerary

RECALL THAT most efficient and effective healing protocol initially releases blockages of greatest relative density and, thereafter, releases blockages of relative subtlety. Observe this cadence. Practice daily for ninety days. The Menu may gradually shift – but do not practice any vertical activity for less than thirty days. Activities must be practiced no less than three times (days) per week. You must use vertical activities that influence the six senses (including etheric sense). See the Menu above for recommended exercises. Keep a Daily Journal to record all noteworthy daily observations (regarding intuition, dreams, synchronicity . . . and miracles). As psyche' requires rhythm for growth, it is preferable to perform a specific activity at the same time daily, during each day of practice.

SCHEDULE OF SOUL-ALIGNED ACTIVITY (VERTICALITY)

Every Moment
As Often as Necessary
Upon Waking
Commuting / Driving
Morning
Lunch (At Meals)
Commuting / Driving
Evening
Pre-Sleep
Nutrition Plan
Miscellaneous
Journal (Emotions, Intuition, Synchronicity, Dreams ... and Miracles)

A SAMPLE ITINERARY
(90-Day Program)

Every Moment
Mindfulness (Intend presence in every moment)
Body-Centered Breath (Abdominal Breath)

As Often As Necessary
Body-Centered Breathing (Foot Breath, Emotional Release)
Qi Gong Therapy
Hydration

Morning (1 hour)
Flower Essences (varies), Aromatherapy (varies)
Oils (Frankincense, Myrrh, Sandalwood)
Body-Centered Breath (Fire Breath)
Symbology (Japanese/Reiki, Kabbalah)
Mantra (Hindu)
Om Nama Shiviah (the Infinite)
Om Hraum Mitraya Namaha (Aligned Community)
Prayer (Christian)
BodyWork (Qi Nei Tsang, Taoist Internal Organ Manipulation)
Yoga (Ashtanga practice – 10 to 60 minutes)
Standing Meditation (Qi Gong)
Dragon & Tiger Qi Gong (10 – 20 minutes)
Stillness Meditation (12 – 60 minutes)
Journal (Emotions, Dreams, Synchronicity, Intuition; … and Miracles)
Creative Writing
Create Music

Driving
Abdominal Breath, Vertical Breath (Heaven and Earth Breathing)
Symbols (Kabbalah)
Toning (Om)
Mantra

At Meals
Blessing of Food (and companions, ingredients, natural elements)
Hand Chakra Connection to Food

Evening
Cardio (20 – 40 minutes)
Work Out (30 – 60 minutes)

Diet
No beef, no chicken, minimal caffeine and sugar, maximize water

Miscellaneous
Call a friend each day (that you have not talked to in a while)

*   *   *

BIOGRAPHY

ANDREW SADOCK RESIDES IN CHICAGO. During summers, he serves as tall ship owner and captain of the *Red Witch*. During winters, he serves as a holistic life coach/consultant, energyworker, qi gong instructor, motivational lecturer, and performing musician.

Mr. Sadock completed a PhD dissertation in 2012. His intention is to serve as a professor to introduce a curriculum of holistic philosophy/psychology/energetic medicine to universities adapted from four books he has written. Additionally, he intends to create a non-profit foundation to serve underprivileged children by presenting a daily boot camp aboard tall ships (Chicago and Los Angeles).

He practiced holistic energywork and bodywork in Chicago, San Francisco, and at Esalen Institute (Big Sur, California). He wrote three books regarding holistic philosophy, psychology, and energetics (published by Amazon, Lulu, and Barnes & Noble. He has also created a screenplay adapted from a book regarding a true tale of synchronicity.

Mr. Sadock's background includes experience as a child advocate, architectural tour-boat captain, licensed massage therapist, MBA, CPA, composer, lyricist, guitarist, sitarist, bassist, vocalist, sailor, motorcyclist, rugby player, and college rugby coach. He attended Washington University (St. Louis, MO).

Mr. Sadock is author of several books and a screenplay, in addition to having recorded music designed to enhance vibration, such as his CDs *Yin* and *Yang*. Further information is available through his website, AndrewSadock.com.

CONTACT INFORMATION
Andrew@AndrewSadock.com
AndrewSadock.com
773.439.0948